T0243126

45th Anniversary Edition

UFO . . . Contact from the Pleiades

Volumes I & II

The amazing photo-events and photo-experiences from the most startling case of ongoing alien contact to appear in modern history.

Brit Elders, Lee Elders, Thom Welch

Photo identification by Wendelle C. Stevens, USAF Ret.

BEYOND WORDS

Portland, Oregon

UFO...Contact from the Pleiades, *Volume I* and *Volume II* were released years ago, while the case was still being investigated. There may be statements made in present tense that pertain to that time.

BEYOND WORDS
1750 S.W. Skyline Blvd, Suite 20
Portland, Oregon 97221-2543
503-531-8700 / 503-531-8773 fax
www.beyondword.com

First Beyond Words hardcover edition April 2024

First published by Genesis III Publishing: Volume I (978-0-93785-002-2) published in 1979 and Volume II (LCCN 80133014) published in 1983

BEYOND WORDS PUBLISHING and colophon are registered trademarks of Beyond Words Publishing. Beyond Words is an imprint of Simon & Schuster, LLC.

For more information about special discounts for bulk purchases, please contact Beyond Words Special Sales at 503-531-8700 or specialsales@beyondwords.com.

Managing editor: Lindsay Easterbrooks-Brown
Copyeditor: Bailey Potter
Proofreader: Kristin Thiel
Illustrations: Eduard "Billy" Meier, Lt. Col. Wendelle C. Stevens, USAF Ret., Lee Elders, Brit Elders
Design: Sara Blum, Devon Smith

Manufactured in China

10 9 8 7 6 5 4 3

Library of Congress Control Number: 2023950166

ISBN 978-1-58270-911-6 (hardcover)
ISBN 978-1-58270-928-4 (eBook)

The corporate mission of Beyond Words Publishing, Inc.: *Inspire to Integrity*

For Lee and Wendelle, two dedicated men who always hoped these books would be combined so that the thought-provoking wonder and beauty of this enigmatic case could be experienced together by future generations. And for all those whose minds are open enough to create a question and seek an answer.

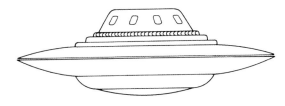

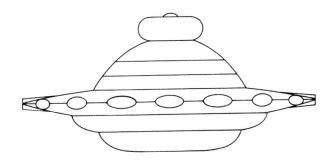

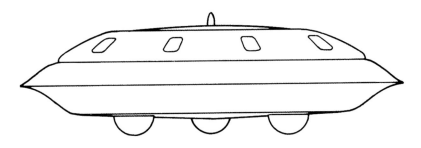

Contents

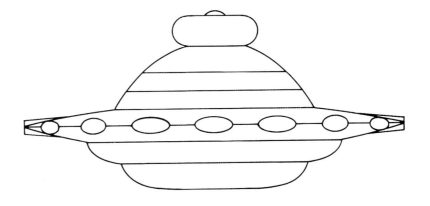

Preface

As you turn the pages of the book, you are stepping back decades to a time when life seemed less complicated. Technology was just beginning to enter our personal lives. In the mid-'70s, most people weren't interested in what inventor Ed Roberts called "Personal Computers." His Altair 8800 was sold as a kit. It weighed about 55 pounds, had a five-inch CRT display screen, a tape drive, a 1.9 MHz PALM processor, and 64 KB of RAM. Once assembled, the box-shaped machines didn't have keyboard, color monitor, or video terminal. There was no software, and programming was done in assembly language.

The year 1977 ushered in the breakthrough computer companies of Commodore, Tandy, and Apple that introduced color graphics to the computing world. Laptops, tablets, and smart phones were years away from reality.

Digital photography was in its infancy, and it took a studio like Industrial Light and Magic, which launched in 1975, to produce the stunning visual effects we then saw in movie theaters.

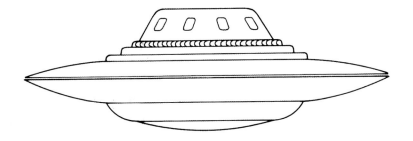
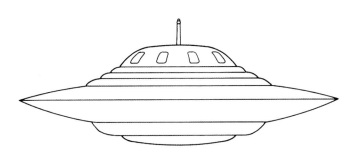

Prologue

It was a morning in November 1983 when I visited my friend Roberto Martin, an engineer who had built an amazing house that was completely self-sufficient, which in those days was not only rare but also exemplary. Roberto's home produced its own energy and captured and stored its own rainwater, and they generated their own food by farming the land. This remarkable house was located in the middle of a forest on the outskirts of Mexico City, at more than three thousand meters above sea level. It was, without a doubt, a development that was ahead of its time. That was where my life changed.

After I toured the place in the company of fellow Mexican television journalists, Roberto decided to show us a book with large color photographs about an investigation that had been carried out by Lee and Brit Elders, Col. Wendelle Stevens, and Thom Welch. From the first moment I saw the book, I could not take my eyes off the amazing images that were shown in the publication.

I just started to babble, "Is this real?" The answer was immediate. With his deep and dominant voice, Roberto replied, "Of course, the investigation proves it, and not only is it real, but it is extraordinary."

The images presented ships with extraterrestrial characteristics such as I had never seen in my life. I went through the pages of the book about the case of a Swiss farmer named Eduard "Billy" Meier. There were all the details, there was talk of other witnesses, analysis of the metals of the ships, recorded sounds, expert evidence of the photographs, and sounds of the ships. The case seemed to leave no doubt as to its authenticity.

I dared to borrow the book for a few days, since I thought it could be investigated and presented on the Mexican television program *60 Minutes*, a very popular and highly credible news program of which I was the editor general. Roberto Martin not only agreed to lend me his valuable copy but he offered me another book that had been written by just Col. Stevens that included additional information on this case.

The story was truly fascinating. According to Col. Stevens, the Swiss farmer, Meier, maintained contact with beings from the Pleiades, who had a physical appearance very similar to ours. The cosmonaut responded to the name Semjase (pronounced Sem-YA'see), and the most impressive thing was that they had given him (Meier) messages. One of the messages from the Pleiades was that the most important reason for their mission to Earth was that a hole would be opening in the Earth's ozone layer due to the inert gases released by human beings.

The message that a hole would be opening in the ozone layer was given to Meier on January 28, 1975. It was a warning that would be confirmed in 1985 and made known to the world in 1986, when British scientists working in Halley Bay, Antarctica, discovered that the hole in the ozone layer was real.

Everything in this case seemed to be supported by evidence—a fundamental element for an investigative journalist—so I decided to propose to *60 Minutes* that an investigation be carried out on the case and presented on Mexican TV.

Not without some inconvenience and rejection, I was eventually able to convince my superiors to investigate and present this case. It was broadcast on Mexican television on March 18, 1984, under the title "In the Sea of the Universe." Despite it having been broadcast after midnight, the impact on Mexican society was impressive. The investigation was rebroadcast a few weeks later due to the extraordinary response that was generated, and copies of the program were made and circulated in different Spanish-speaking countries for years.

It was possible to prove that each of the evidences presented was real, the analyses done by experts, and the work carried out by Lee and Brit Elders was nothing short of extraordinary.

From that moment, without my having intended it, my name was synonymous with the phenomenon of the extraterrestrial visitations.

Despite my reluctance to get involved more deeply with the subject, I was invited to make two debate programs in 1991 on the television series *Usted que Opnia* hosted by Nino Canún. I did not want my journalism to be labeled by and limited to this topic. I agreed to appear, and as expected, everything changed.

From the success of the Nino Canún programs, where the first clear videos of a UFO were presented, a maelstrom began that has followed me to this day.

Almost forty years later, I was able to bring together a team of researchers who specialized in the subject, and today we hold a two-hour weekly program dedicated to the subject on Mexican TV and the internet. It's broadcast nationally during prime time on Sundays and has generated the largest collection of videos worldwide on the subject. It's recognized for the awakening of several generations of human beings to a subject that today is finally been considered authentic. Our hope is that very soon communication with other beings will begin.

It all started that morning in November 1983, thanks to the meticulous research work of Lee and Brit Elders, who became two of my dearest friends. From them I learned the importance of this topic and also the professionalism necessary in the research to get involved in such a difficult subject.

My life changed that morning, and at every step, the importance of this topic has reaffirmed that of the visitation of nonhumans to our planet means, without a doubt, the possibility of unification and change so necessary for humanity.

My dear friend Lee is no longer with us; however, Brit, his lifelong partner, has decided to re-present the Pleiadian/Billy Meier story of contact—a case that is as current today as it was decades ago when I first heard of it.

Surely this story will continue to change the lives of countless people who, like me, will encounter the extraordinary reality of being just one of the civilizations that inhabit the Universe.

—**Jaime Maussan**,
award-wining journalist,
investigative reporter, and television host
Mexico City, 2024

Foreword

One of the star beings cases that I find most credible and fascinating is the Billy Meier case in Switzerland. Lee and Brit Elders investigated that case for years, and with them, I visited Billy at his home in 1981. For about two weeks I walked the contact sites, met many of the witnesses, and listened to his stories about his contacts and conversations with the female Pleiadian cosmonaut Semjase.

My time with Billy was mind-bending. I never saw the crafts while I was there, but many of the local villagers, both children and adults, had. We talked day and night, and I recorded the majority of our conversations. Billy told me how his life had changed, how it was no longer simple, and how it had negatively affected his family and himself. He said that disreputable people had stolen some of the pictures he had taken of the craft, others tried to start disinformation campaigns against him, and there had even been several assassination attempts on his life. Because of these and other human interactions, he looked forward to the peaceful dialogues he had with his otherworldly friends.

Semjase told him that her star people experienced the same severe problems and monumental decisions facing us on Earth, approximately thirty centuries ago. They have since evolved in knowledge, social structure, science, and technology with the help of more advanced beings than themselves. She said that they are far from being perfect and are always evolving, just as we are. Semjase also told him that if we genuinely pooled all of our intelligence and imagination toward peace, we could achieve their level of evolvement in a few hundred years, but we have to take the first step of recognizing that we are not alone in the universe.

The Pleiades' primary reason for communicating with Billy and supplying the physical evidence was for the purpose of creating an awareness that other intelligent life exists in the universe, both good and bad by our standards, human and nonhuman in form.

—**Shirley MacLaine**,
award-winning actress and bestselling author
Santa Fe, New Mexico, 2024

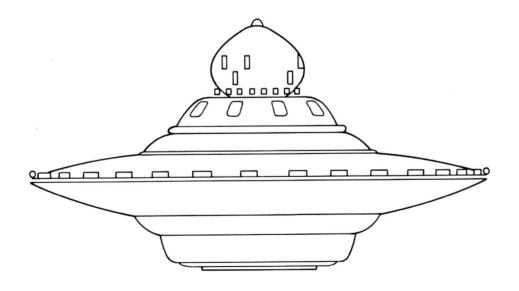

Introduction

Until the mid-'70s, the most prominent UFO case was the 1961 abduction case of Betty and Barney Hill. On their way home to Portsmouth, New Hampshire, they noticed a bright object in the night sky that was moving erratically. The object grew brighter and brighter until it descended right in front of the car.

The couple stated that they had experienced an altered state of consciousness that blurred their memories but that, once they regained full consciousness, they realized they had traveled about thirty-five miles with no recollection of the journey. Two days after the encounter, Betty called Pease Air Force Base to report the incident.

After restless, uneasy days spent trying to determine what had happened to them and why they had "missing time" and dreams that could be described as night terrors, the couple agreed to undergo hypno-regression therapy. The Hills didn't know who had taken them, or why, but under hypnosis, they recalled seeing what they called "a star map" and being frightened by beings that did not look human.

The Hills did not try to hide their encounter nor did they actively seek publicity. They spoke, as candidly as possible, to researchers and investigators, and eventually there were books and movies made about their experience, which brought the topic of UFOs and possible abductions into vernacular of the mainstream media.

Many people had heard of Project Blue Book and of the Roswell incident but there were few places to report sightings. APRO, CUFOS, and MUFON were the primary organizations that gathered information on the phenomena, but sightings still went unreported. One of the most notable was that of US President Jimmy Carter (1977–1981). In 1969 he shared with friends that he had seen an unidentified flying object in Leary, Georgia, but it wasn't until 1973 that the future president made an official report to the International UFO Bureau in Oklahoma.

Abduction cases did happen, but they were far fewer than sightings of anomalous objects. The most significant, besides the Hills' experience, were Charles Hickson and Calvin Parker (two fisherman on the Pascagoula River, Mississippi), Arizona forestry worker Travis Walton, and farmer Jan Wolski of Emilcin, Poland, where a monument was erected to commemorate the event.

As with all of these experiences—both sightings and abductions—there were believers and skeptics. A conclusion in either direction was reached based on someone's account of an incident. Physical evidence left in the wake of the event was limited, which left a gap in information, especially where science was concerned. Some reports made national news, but their notoriety was basically limited to those intrigued by the subject. Debate of the validity of an observance or encounter by those who were not directly involved fueled the topic for a few news cycles and then faded back into obscurity.

The Pleiadian contact case was different. In the mid-'70s, the European print media swarmed around this case that took place in a rural part of Switzerland because it has something other cases did not present: physical documentation.

A one-armed Swiss man claimed contact with beings that looked quite human and, he stated, came from the star system Pleiades. Not only had he met with them but he had been allowed to take photographs and 8mm movie footage of the crafts, been given metal samples, and recorded audio of the crafts, and, remarkably, dozens of witnesses had watched the unidentified aerial craft coming and going from the contacts. He had also written up his recollection of the conversations that had taken place.

Lt. Col. Wendelle C. Stevens, USAF (retired), had been an enthusiastic researcher of the subject since his time in the Air Force, where he served in the once-classified Ptarmigan Project based in Alaska. Col. Stevens was part of the strategic aerial reconnaissance unit, which utilized aircraft to collect photographic and electronic information. The material collected was then flown to Washington, DC where it was analyzed.

As a pilot, Col. Stevens was always interested in aircraft design. His interest in UFOs was piqued by fellow pilots who shared stories of unidentified objects that flew higher and faster than they could, made right-angle turns, and vanished in an instant. Familiar with all types of aircraft in service at that time, he was amazed at the flight capabilities described by his colleagues. That, and his perpetual curiosity, spurred a lifelong interest in the phenomena.

He had amassed an enormous private collection of images of and stories about unusual airships from all parts of the globe. The observers were from all walks of life, from police to farmers to teachers to politicians, and none of them could identify the object they had seen or photographed or the flight characteristics it had displayed. The aircrafts varied in size, color, and shape and were described as cigar-shaped, disc-shaped, top-shaped, or round orbs. Each of the observers was equally adamant that they had seen a UFO—an unidentified flying object.

As Col. Stevens continued to delve into the enigmatic topic, his friends Lee and Brit Elders were maintaining an expanding electronic counter measure (ECM) company that they had founded with their friend, Thom Welch. For years Lee had spent half the year living with the Shuar, an Indigenous ethnic group inhabiting the jungles of Ecuador, and half the year working as a private investigator with his friend, Thom. During a lengthy corporate espionage investigation, they realized there was a need, in both the corporate and the private sectors, for an ECM company that could protect against illegal wiretapping and eavesdropping.

After researching the best technology available at the time, the three formed Intercep and purchased and were trained on how to use the state-of-the-art telephone analyzer and RF (radio frequency) detection equipment. The company's reputation grew because they never divulged a client's name and even created specialized bank accounts to prevent nonessential personnel from knowing Intercep had secured the phone and computer lines and premises. They trained and employed former law enforcement officers and military personnel to assist in sweeps, and the only reference they gave was a former attorney general for the state of Arizona. Because of their knowledge and confidentiality, they grew their clientele to include Fortune 500 companies, international corporations, banks, major league sports organizations, as well as attorneys and private individuals.

The Elderses were aware of Col. Stevens's penchant for UFO stories but were surprised when he asked them to meet with a woman from Switzerland who had quite a story to tell.

They arrived at his home to find Col. Stevens and a small silver-haired woman huddled over his dining room table, which was covered with photograph albums, loose papers, and notebooks. In the center of the table were photographs that depicted a lush, green countryside with a silvery, disc-shaped object hovering above the ground.

Col. Stevens excitedly introduced the Elderses to Lou Zinsstag, who had traveled from her home in Switzerland to tell him about an extraterrestrial contact case. She explained that a man who had had face-to-face contacts with the occupants of the craft took the photographs and had other physical evidence. The photographs were not of the typical hazy objects so often seen in UFO images. They were impressive, crystal clear, and at first glance, too good to be true.

The four spent the afternoon discussing the case, and after Ms. Zinsstag left, Col. Stevens suggested that, in his estimation, this situation was too big for a typical UFO group and suggested that it would require the type of investigation that Intercep could provide. It would require personnel who were well-equipped and knowledgeable in techniques and technology. Lee quickly vetoed the idea. He had worked too hard to throw the solid reputation of a thriving company into something as intangible as a UFO case.

Col. Stevens was fascinated by the reported events and said he would go to meet the man, see the evidence, and return with an objective opinion, but when he returned, he was anything but objective. Brit Elders kept a daily journal and noted that Stevens had returned an "obsessed man." He had always believed that the majority of sightings were of extraterrestrial origin. Despite what Project Blue Book indicated, he didn't believe swamp gas and other natural anomalies were the basis of the images he had seen and stories he had been told. To him, the Pleiadian contact case had the potential to dispel those generally accepted theories.

Three things made the Pleiadian contact case unique:

1) Unlike abduction cases, these events were agreed to by both parties, making it a contact case,
2) It happened frequently, not just once, and
3) There was physical evidence that could be analyzed to support or contradict the individual's claims.

He reported that there were photographs, though many had been stolen or misplaced, 8mm movie footage, metal samples, witnesses, landing tracks, notes from the contacts, and recorded sounds of the spacecraft. Meier, whom in Col. Stevens's estimation was a simple man who worked as a night watchman to support his wife and three children, had impressed him. Over the next few months, Stevens continued to plead his case and tried to enlist Intercep in the investigation. Lee continued to decline any involvement.

Intercep was gaining an international reputation, and the business was expanding rapidly. Thom Welch had been invited to speak at the Honeywell Computer Security and Privacy Symposium to be held in April 1978. The Elderses were arranging several meetings in Europe while Stevens continued to push for their involvement. Finally, the Elderses agreed to take a look—only because they had a client in London and Switzerland was just a short flight away.

In April 1978, the Elderses and Stevens arrived at the Swiss farmhouse where Meier and his family lived. Melting snow had turned the driveway to the house into a river of mud. A shutter on an upstairs window hung askew, and the exterior of the home desperately needed paint and repair. Inside was not much better. The roof leaked, and there was no indoor plumbing or central heating. Kalliope, Meier's wife, was boiling water to wash dishes, and the smell of fresh-baked bread filled the room.

In the kitchen around a large table was a local television crew interviewing Meier and a number of witnesses. What remained of Meier's arm, amputated after a bus accident in Turkey, rested on a small, gray fleece pillow as he listened intently to the interviewers. With no hesitance he took a sip of strong black coffee from a delicate demitasse cup and directly answered the questions being posed by the journalists. He flashed a broad, welcoming smile to the Americans and invited them to join the others seated around the table.

The interactions of everyone at the table gave the Elderses an opportunity to observe Meier, his family, and the other witnesses. There were no obvious nonverbal clues from Meier; his vocal tone and posture remained unchanged. His facial expressions remained consistent with the answers he was providing. The Elderses noted that he referred to the spacecraft as a "beamship" and said one of his Pleiadian contacts was a woman named Semjase.

His three young children demanded the attention of their mother, which she quietly provided as she ushered them from the room. The witnesses seated at the table included a pilot, an attorney, and two teachers. Each candidly related a few of their experiences to the television crew who seemed anxious to get back to the station to edit the footage. They quickly concluded their time with Meier, shaking hands and wishing everyone well.

Lee Elders expected to be able to quickly discern how this Swiss man had faked everything and leave. But, after spending several days with Meier—walking and measuring the locations where the photographs had been taken, reviewing the images, speaking with the witnesses, exploring the farmhouse and surrounding area, and spending long nights in the kitchen questioning Meier—the Elderses knew this was not going to be a quick and easy investigation. They had found no models stashed anywhere on the property, no sign of deception from Meier, the family, or the other witnesses, and there were even surrounding neighbors who reported seeing unusual lights in the night skies.

The day before the Americans were to leave for the States, Meier joined them in the kitchen. He set a tattered pink shoebox before him on the table and removed the lid. He smiled as he removed three 35mm photographic canisters and said in a thick Swiss accent, "In here are stages of the metal of the beamships." He placed about half of the contents of each film canister into three empty containers and handed them to Lee. As the day progressed, Meier also provided the Elderses with audio recordings of the beamship, the names and contact information of the other witnesses, and prints and internegatives of many of the images, which he said were closest to the originals. The Elderses agreed to take the evidence back to the US and see what could be learned from it.

Thus began a seven-year investigation that spanned three continents, dozens of laboratories, and specialists from a variety of disciplines.

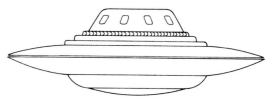

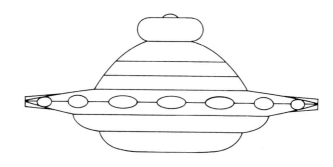

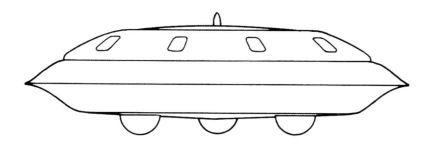

Volume I

"We, too, are still far removed from perfection and have to evolve constantly, just like yourselves. We are neither superior nor superhuman, nor are we missionaries...We feel duty bound to the citizens of Earth, because our forefathers were your forefathers..."

—**Semjase**, Pleiadian cosmonaut, February 8, 1975

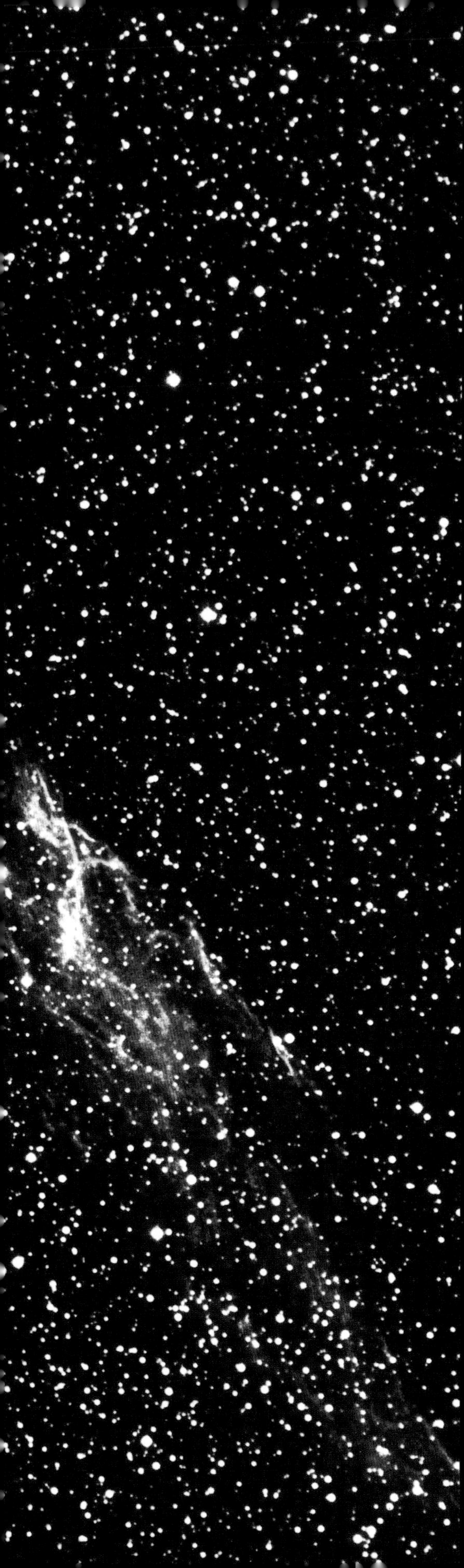

"If the intelligence of these [UFO] creatures were sufficiently superior to ours, they might choose to have little, if any contact with us."

—**Brookings Institute**, in a report on extraterrestrial life,
New York Times, December 15, 1960

"The masses would merely revere us as gods, as in ages past, or go off in hysteria, that is why we regard it prudent to make contact with individual persons only for the time being, in order to disseminate, through them the knowledge concerning our existence and our coming to this planet."

—**Semjase**, Pleiadian cosmonaut, February 8, 1975

"There were men from the sky in the earth in these days."

—*Hebrew Book of Light*, twelfth to thirteenth centuries

"Mankind are here because they are the offspring of parents who were first brought here from another planet. And power was given them to propagate their species. And they were commanded to multiply and replenish the earth."

—**Brigham Young**, *Journal of Discourses*, Vols. 7–8, 1860

"I can assure you that flying saucers, given that they exist, are not constructed by any power on earth."

—**President Harry S. Truman**, press conference, April 4, 1950

"Something unknown to our understanding is visiting this earth."

—**Dr. Mitrovan Zverev**, Soviet scientist, August 1965

"These objects (UFO) are conceived and directed by intelligent beings of a very high order. They probably do not originate in our solar system, perhaps not even in our galaxy."

—**Dr. Hermann Oberth**, internationally renowned rocket and
space travel authority and often called the father
of the V-1 and V-2 weaponry of World War II,
press conference, Innsbruck, Austria, June 1954

"In the distant future we will encounter some other intelligent life."

—**Frank Borman**, astronaut, *Pomona Progress Bulletin*, 1971

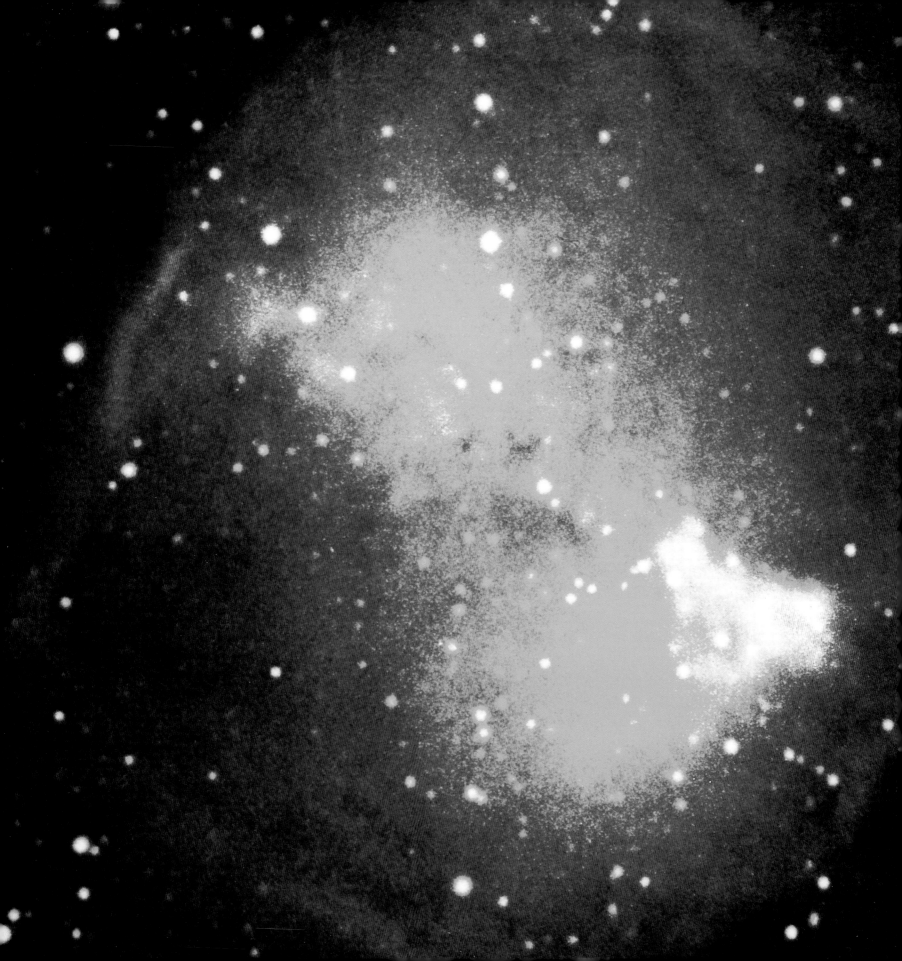

The heaven by night is full of marvels…There is "the evening star,"
Hesperus fairest of the stars, "sharer of the throne of Aphrodite"—
why so, lovers know well. There is the group of seven stars, the Pleiades;
they are as it were the nymphs of heaven. As "doves" (Pleiades)
they bring to Zeus ambrosia; yet at the same time they are comely goddesses,
daughters of the Titan Atlas, and spouses of the gods…*

* Tadeusz Zieliński, *The Religion of Ancient Greece* (United Kingdom: Oxford University Press, H. Milford, 1926), 28–29.

ORION

THE HYADES

THE PLEIADES

The Taurus Section of our skies

The Pleiades

"When the skies are searched for signals from extraterrestrial civilizations, search carefully in the Pleiades."
— **Irwin Ginsburgh, PhD**, *First, Man. Then, Adam!*

A cluster of stars known throughout history as the Seven Sisters or the Daughters of Zeus—Maia, Electra, Celaeno, Taygeta, Asterope, Merope, and Alcyone—also mothers of Greek gods, are believed to have been turned into stars by Zeus so that they might be safe from Orion, who had chased them for seven years. There are no stars so widely acclaimed as these; their beauty and grace are spoken of in literature from all cultures, past and present.

Sappho, Euripides, and Homer referred to the Pleiades in their writings. Later, in the Rubaiyat written by the poet-astronomer Omar Khayyam in 1123, they were referred to as "the Begetters, as beginning all things," while half a world away, an ancient Peruvian legend identified the Pleiades uniquely as the "arbiters of human destiny." In China they were worshipped by young women as the Seven Sisters of Industry and in ancient times were known as Mol, the constellation Or Gang. Milton called them the "Seven Atlantic Sisters;" Manly P. Hall, in *The Secret Teaching of All Ages*, stated that "the sacred Pleiades were famous to freemasonry as the Seven Stars at the upper end of The Sacred Ladder." As the Seven Sisters they are familiar to most, and as the Seven Stars they are one of the few star clusters mentioned throughout the Bible.

"The Pleiades seem to be among the first stars mentioned in astronomical literature, appearing in Chinese annals of 2357 B.C."
— **Robert B. Baker**, *Introducing the Constellations*

The German astronomer Bessel stated that the Pleiades are literally a cluster of suns drifting together in one direction, led by the brightest of the seven, Alcyone, which the early Arabs referred to as Al Jauzah or Al Wasat, the Central One. And it has been noted that Alcyone shines to its sister stars with eighty-three times the brilliance of Sirius and that its brilliancy is one thousand times greater than that of our sun.

No other area of the sky has been investigated as often and as carefully as that containing the Pleiades. A small two-inch telescope was used in 1664 by Robert Hooke, who counted seventy-eight individual stars in this group. In 1876

This photograph of the constellation Taurus shows the Pleiades to the right of the Orion and Hyades star groups, as normally seen in the night sky of the northern hemisphere without the aid of a telescope. Courtesy of O. Richard Norton, astronomer, this photograph represents a seventy-degree field and was taken at Kitt Peak Observatory outside Tucson, Arizona, using a 28mm f2.8 Cannon lens on a 35mm Cannon SLR camera. The Ecktachrome ASA 400 film (later pushed to 1600 ASA) was exposed for two minutes.

The Experience: The Beginning

"You call us extraterrestrials or star-men, and you attribute to us superhuman powers even though you do not know us. Regarding this, we are men, like you, but our knowledge and our understanding exceeds yours considerably, especially in the technical field."

—**Semjase**, Pleiadian cosmonaut, 1975

(Sem-YA'see)

Tuesday, January 28, 1975
14:12 hours
The Swiss countryside of Hinwel

As Mr. Meier looked across the empty road toward the meadow and forest beyond, noting to himself how remote they seemed…suddenly it began…

Meier heard a very unusual sound. A low, throbbing, humming sound that defied description. Then he saw it—a strange, silver disc-shaped craft circling slowly above. He couldn't believe his eyes!

He recovered just in time to take several quick photographs, almost forgetting the camera was there, before the strange craft swooped down and softly landed in the clearing one hundred meters away. About seven meters in diameter, it just sat there quietly.

With adrenaline pumping, Mr. Meier ran excitedly toward it, but without warning, he was arrested by an unknown force within fifty meters of the craft. It was like trying to advance in a hurricane wind, a strong barrier, invisible in nature. Then, from behind the craft, the cosmonaut came, walking directly toward him. Meier strained his eyes in disbelief!

His first contact with the Pleiadians had begun.

March 18, 1975, 09:07 hours
Winkelriet, Switzerland
Photograph taken by Eduard "Billy" Meier prior to the eighth contact as craft approached.

Eduard "Billy" Meier, a Swiss farmer/caretaker and father of three, had left his farmhouse because of an odd compulsion to take his camera and leave—that's the only way that he could describe it. As he had driven his moped curiously through the countryside, following the unusual thought patterns that seemed so strong, Mr. Meier had no way of knowing that within hours his experience would produce historic evidence of extraterrestrial intelligence surpassing anything ever seen by modern civilization surviving on the only planet believed to support life in the Universe.

15:58 hours

As he watched the cosmonaut return to the disc-shaped craft, an incredulous Mr. Meier pondered the words of this strange visitor. He noted that the time had seemed to pass so quickly. The craft disappeared for a moment behind a flare of energy as it began to move. He wanted it to stay as thousands of questions raced through his mind. The cosmonaut had mentioned that there would be other meetings, but the possibility of this being the last kept his thoughts racing and heightened his desire to remember every detail.

The craft continued to rise, now clearly visible with a reddish-blue light appearing to radiate completely around its outer edge. Mr. Meier quickly snapped a picture and then lost sight of the craft. For a moment he felt disappointed, but as he waited, straining his eyes in hopes of following the craft's departure, the silver disc returned.

The spaceship had a very smooth metallic surface unbroken by seams, lines, openings, or projections except for the "ports" around its dome. Its surface had a degree of translucence to it and appeared silvery or goldish silver at rest, yet the metallic finish seemed to go through color changes in flight. Having no markings or emblems of any kind, its surface seemed highly polished and reflected the sunlight brilliantly. In a fraction of a second, these observations were struck into memory with the exhilaration of the moment. Mr. Meier snapped a final picture as the craft turned overhead, and he watched it suddenly flash away out of sight, ending the experience as quickly as it began.

While slowly walking back to his moped, Mr. Meier couldn't help thinking about how these incredible moments had started earlier in the day, with those strange, compelling feelings and those "thought-pictures" that had led him all the way here. The cosmonaut had told him to pay attention to such feelings, as they would indicate another meeting was at hand.

Time after time, he followed these same impulses in the ensuing months, returning home after each event with rolls and rolls of undeveloped film and reports of phenomenally detailed conversations with beings from the star system known to us as the Pleiades. These unworldly meetings took place at all hours of the day and night, leaving substantial evidence in their wake, including hundreds of remarkably clear photographs, landing tracks, burned bushes, recorded 8mm film footage, sound recordings of the sleek spacecraft in flight, physical samples, and over a dozen eyewitnesses who would substantiate his story, some having filmed portions of the events themselves.

Billy Meier's experiences have become the longest series of documented encounters ever recorded. By April 4, 1978, he had a total of 105 meetings with the Pleiadian cosmonauts, and the ongoing events continued to produce remarkable new photographs and a host of unparalleled evidence.

March 8, 1975, 17:20 hours
Distance to tree line: 350 yards
Location: Ober-Sadelegg

As the Pleiadians left many of these meetings, their crafts were observed by numerous witnesses who were astounded at the reality of the claimed events. These eye-opening experiences of others created needed support for the quiet Swiss farmer whose sanity was previously questioned at the mere mention of these encounters he was experiencing. But such was the nature of the events as first reported. As the encounters continued and attention on them increased, the quiet rural communities of Canton Zurich, Switzerland, were forever disturbed by the historical proportions of experiences they could no longer ignore.

Billy Meier kept a careful log of notes on the contacts: times, places, dates, detailed conversations, comments, witnesses, and the important highlights underscored by the Pleiadians themselves. The physical meetings with the returning spacecraft and its occupants were occurring once or twice a month, and with each new meeting a stronger friendship and understanding developed with the cosmonauts.

Having observed our progress for thousands of years, the Pleiadian visitors had observations and studies that were detailed in these numerous unworldly conversations. Technical, social, historical, and many spiritual subject matters were discussed in the process of answering the thousands of questions Mr. Meier had.

Since they were Nordic-looking with few physical differences from our own form, Meier felt very comfortable. The farmer had no difficulty conversing with Semjase and the other alien crew members when they visited, because they understood his questions and problems before he mentioned them. They were telepathic. But they also spoke to him in his native Swiss-German dialect, with an unusual accent.

"We, too, learn the various languages of your planet, but it is much easier for us than for you because we have simpler methods. We are in possession of all Earth-languages, which are spoken at the moment or have ever been spoken in past ages. We have exact data on them from which we have developed language courses. This happens through a computer-like apparatus under the supervision of language experts or specialized scientists assigned to our task force. Other types of apparatus may serve to connect us to the computer in such a way to make it virtually possible for the languages to be inspired into us, as it were, and this is done while we assume a hypnotic-like condition. The entire course lasts about twenty-one days (of Earth time). Following this, we require another approximate ten days of advanced training in order to become fluent in the language selected. . . . We then practice in free conversation with a language scientist before we enter into contact with terrestrials."

—**Semjase**, Pleiadian cosmonaut, 1975

Location: near Rumlikon, Berg, and Theilingen
This sighting was a filming event only. The seven-meter (twenty-one-foot) spacecraft moved from left to right across the beautiful panorama. Some 8mm motion pictures were also taken. Mr. Meier took all of the still photographs on his Olympus 35 ECR camera having an F 42mm, 2.8 lens. The lens was jammed just short of infinity because of previous damage, thus hampering the focus of some photographs.

Semjase told Mr. Meier that they had long ago experienced the same difficult problems and decisions our world now faced, and they had evolved approximately thirty centuries ahead of Earth society in knowledge, social structure, and science, with the help of beings more advanced than themselves. Their purpose now focused upon creating an awareness that other intelligent life existed in the universe, both good and bad by our standards, human and nonhuman in form.

"We, too, are still far removed from perfection and have to evolve constantly, just like yourselves. We are neither superior nor superhuman, nor are we missionaries…but we have taken on certain tasks such as, for example, the supervision of developing life in space, particularly human, and to ensure a certain measure of order. In the course of these duties, we do here and there approach the denizens of various worlds, select some individuals, and instruct them. This we do only when a race is in a stage of higher evolution. Then we explain (and prove) to them that they are not the only thinking beings in the universe."

—**Semjase**, Pleiadian cosmonaut, 1975

"Several times we have tried to establish contact with terrestrial humans who might want to assist us in our task. We opened contact, but the men selected gave evidence of not being sufficiently willing or loyal. Others were afraid of their own kind (fellow men) and permitted our contacts to go unreported. They explained that their own kind would consider them liars or mad or would destroy their existence with intrigues.

"The terrestrials of many organizations are busy studying our spacecraft, but they did not always have available authentic photographs. Some are luminous effects accidentally photographed; others are down-right falsifications…We are giving you the opportunity of taking photographs of our spaceships, and other similar opportunities will be afforded you so that you may obtain better photographs, be it technically or artistically than now exist."

—**Semjase**, Pleiadian cosmonaut, 1975

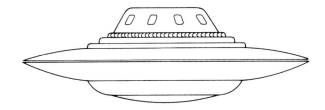

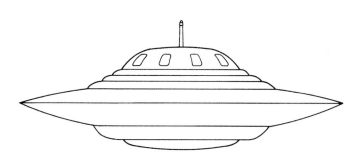

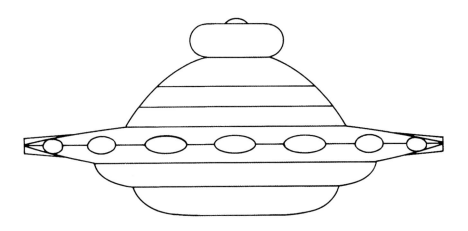

"A single second in the timeless amounts to many million years in normal space."

—**Ptaah** (P-tah'), Pleiadian cosmonaut, 1975

"We do not reach to an end of the universe, for such does not exist."

—**Semjase**, Pleiadian cosmonaut, 1975

It was from the Pleiades, the Seven Sisters, that these cosmonauts came. They described their home planet, Erra, which orbits a small sun in the system of Taygeta within the giant Pleiades star cluster. They also mentioned the Andromeda Council governing our sector of the universe and the union of planets they belong to, stretching far out into the vastness of space, 127 billion beings strong. Estimating themselves to be three thousand years in advance of Earth, the Pleiadians told Billy Meier that they are not superhuman but like us, benefiting from greater time and greater knowledge.

The Pleiadians told Meier that their civilization began in the constellation of Lyra millions of years past, where it had rapidly reached a high degree of technical progress. The newness of this advanced power created problems and opposing polarities and soon turned brother against brother. Eventually, this forced a thermonuclear war that ultimately destroyed their great society, but not before a major exodus took place. Escapists led by a leader named Pleione (Plā-On-e) fled into space and colonized new homes in the star systems of the Pleiades, the Hyades and Vega. Within a few thousand years, the Pleiadians of Lyran ancestry had founded the new world of Erra, and renewed beam-ship exploration and travel eventually brought them into Earth's solar system ages ago.

Today, the Pleiadians reflect a concern about us, "their younger brothers." If we cannot solve our present problems brought on by the imbalance of our technical advances and ideological differences, we cannot be as fortunate as they, for we presently have no escape routes and no major concern or preparation for this dilemma.

June 12, 1975, 10:38 hours
Location: near Rumlikon, Berg, and Theilingen
Photographs to left and on preceding two-page spread taken by Billy Meier as craft approached—seven-meter, variation type-2 craft. The witness noted that besides moving in curved trajectories, the ship can and often does "jump" instantly from one place to another. Another peculiar thing he observed was a sort of pendulum swing during rapid ascent of the craft. It is erratic, like the descent motions a coin dropped in water exhibits—except in an upward direction. Distance "blueing" by moisture suspended in the air is visible in these pictures, clearly indicating a large object some distance from the camera. Two rolls of thirty-six exposures each were shot in this film series.

"Although terrestrial man may have taken his first step into space, this is still a question of primitive attempts even though he has been able to fly to your moon with missiles. He has still to reach space—because to achieve this end, he needs a force (propulsion) that is able to produce a 'hyperspace' velocity so that the tremendous distances are reduced to something navigable. Then space and time are overcome by non-space and non-time—that is, space and time are reduced almost to annihilation. Through the mastering of this technology, fractions of seconds are sufficient to accomplish light years (of your calculations)…"

—**Semjase**, Pleiadian cosmonaut, 1975

During one of the early contacts, the cosmonauts gave Meier an interesting explanation of their contact method that also offered a reason for the unique cooling sensation he felt across his forehead when such a meeting was imminent.

"After we have selected the individual, we then carefully monitor their thoughts and directly observe their reactions for many years, and then when they have been accepted based on our standards and criteria, we then influence them telepathically to journey into remote locations for direct contact. This is accomplished for several purposes; one is to avoid disturbing other people and causing possible alarm. Also, unless a remote location is used, we have a problem of separating the contactee from other brain wave patterns in the area, a process which normally enables our computer/autopilot to direct our beamship to the exact location without interference.

"...Occasionally, we do not take enough cautionary measures necessary for making the craft unseen. However, even our best measures are not always sufficient. Even at night-time there might be some unexpected observers, which could lead to incidents, especially when we land at a place several times. This might explain the search by the military last week, because they, as well as other authorities, feel in danger when they are informed of sightings or landings of spaceships. Now, we are not the least interested in endangering their power because their tasks pertain to Earth people only."

—**Semjase**, Pleiadian cosmonaut, 1975

The Pleiadians were very adamant in their references of not interfering with the present power structure of our planet, for time and time again they made reference to terrestrial beings as being responsible for their own destiny and the fact that we are solely liable for our own errors and omissions.

March 8, 1975, 17:40 hours
Estimated distance to craft:
one hundred yards
Location: Ober-Sadelegg

26)

"General public contacts are not in our own best interests at this time, and besides, they would not convey a correct significance for the state of mind in which we now exist."

—**Semjase**, Pleiadian cosmonaut, 1975

"On many occasions, space travelers have visited your Earth from other stars (108 different civilizations at last count), sometimes from very distant systems, like ourselves. On occasion, accidental contacts which are unique may take place with Earth people."

—**Semjase**, Pleiadian cosmonaut, 1975

"It now flew completely noiselessly, and I could see the exact form: it was a disc-formed craft with a similar top and base."

—**Eduard "Billy" Meier**, contactee, 1975

"When entering your terrestrial state of existence, we are forced into making a 'slight adjustment' which allows us to function properly within your dimensional world....Therefore this 'connection' ensures a correct state of mind and corresponds with the human vibrational pattern which is necessary for the mutual exchange to take place. It is very similar to your adjusting the fine-tuning dial on your sensitive communication receivers which, when accomplished, allows you perfect reception. In our case, it allows for perfect perception and acclimates us to your physical world of being....This procedure is mandatory for all extra-terrestrial life-forms that visit Earth from other dimensions. Without this slight adjustment, no contacts could take place."

—**Semjase**, Pleiadian cosmonaut, 1975

In a rare glimpse of Pleiadian insight, the beings spoke of Earth mandates that do not conform to their scheme of things…a classic example being Earth time, for they do not measure time by hours or days but instead by events. Thus, they refer to the "event-clock," which not only informs them of our evolutionary progress but also alerts them

On many occasions, the comings and goings of these crafts have been observed and even photographed by a number of other witnesses, many of whom are friends of Billy Meier who, having previously doubted the reality of these fantastic events, had to see it for themselves. Over the years, at least seven different types of spacecrafts have been seen over the Swiss valleys approaching or leaving the contacts with the Swiss farmer. Each type of spacecraft appears in some of the hundreds of photographs Billy Meier has collected of his experience. This photograph shows a variation type-2 craft, an earlier version seen March 8, 1975, which was said to be hundreds of years old.

During Meier's fourth contact, on February 15, 1975, the Pleiadian cosmonauts answered a question regarding the way in which their spacecraft travels to Earth from the Pleiades. Their two different propulsion systems on the spacecraft allow the entire journey to be made in seven hours, with the help of sub-light speeds for atmospheric travel and hyper-space drive systems for travel at many times the speed of light in space.

When asked for more detail, the cosmonauts replied that some of Earth's scientists were working in the proper direction, with some of our top scientists trying out a light-emitting propulsion system (for speeds up to the speed of light) and a "tachyon" system that would enable us to travel many times the speed of light. "We use other names, but the principles are the same," the cosmonauts said.

At the time, these principles mentioned by the cosmonauts could not be generally found scientifically discussed in articles, texts, or books. Then, a full two years later, in a book entitled *Interstellar Travel*, John McVey, a distinguished astronomer, discussed these same propulsion principles. As far as could be determined, John McVey did not know of Eduard "Billy" Meier, and Meier was not familiar with McVey's book.

"We have yet to uncover or document any explainable method Mr. Meier could have had of acquiring these unusual facts, other than through the contacts themselves as he describes."
—**Col. Wendelle Stevens**, 1977

April 14, 1976, 16:15 hours
Location: between Schmarbuel and Mairvinkel
Photograph left, craft moved over the valley from left to right, turned, and then (photograph right) accelerated suddenly toward camera as this photograph was snapped.

"Man should know that the God (force) is quite simply that of creation and that man also, either coming from the higher spiritual spheres or being elevated to those spheres after numerous terrestrial lives, is subject to creation and respectively complementary to it. The higher he soars, the greater becomes his power. However, one can never identify God separately from the creation because God itself is a part of it, with all the rest of the 'Gods' who coexist with it in various states of being, stages of instant celestial substance which are perfectly adapted to them."

—**Semjase**, Pleiadian cosmonaut, 1975

"A spiritually developed being, as a part of creation, acknowledges creation in all things, even the smallest microbe, and leading a creative life causes fears and doubts to vanish like rain before the sun.

"By creative thinking, man acquires knowledge and wisdom and a sense of unlimited strength, which unbinds him from the limitations of convention and dogma. Material life on Earth is only a passing event, a phenomenon vanishing after a time. However, before him and after him, there continues to exist the creative presence of the universe."

—**Semjase**, Pleiadian cosmonaut, 1975

"When the spirit, this universal self, manifests itself in the human being through constant love, wisdom, and truth, then a major breakthrough occurs in the surrounding self-veils which eliminates the physical-material urge of greed, anger, hate, avarice, war....Then and only then has he reached the destination of his existence."

—**Semjase**, Pleiadian cosmonaut, 1975

"And neither is it consistent with the truth that our brothers and sisters come from other parts of space on behalf of a God to bring to the world the long-awaited peace. In no case do we come on behalf of anybody, since creation, by itself, confers no obligation (on us). It is a law unto itself, and every form of life must conform with it and become a part of it."

—**Semjase**, Pleiadian cosmonaut, 1975

March 26, 1976, 16:15 hours
Location: between Bachtelhornli and Unterbactel

On April 14, 1976, Billy made his way to a valley to the west of Bettsroil, anticipating the return of Semjase for another meeting late in the afternoon. He carried a camera and tape recorder with him. Unknown to him, the Swiss Army was on maneuvers to the west in the vicinity of Bettsroil. What happened next is the first time in history that anything like it has been witnessed, tape recorded, and captured on film.

As Semjase's spacecraft approached up the valley preparing to land, the army field radar apparently picked up the spacecraft on their instruments and a Swiss Mirage jet fighter was vectored in to investigate.

The jet fighter came in from the west and made an unsuccessful pass in pursuit of the spacecraft, and the aerial combat maneuvers began. Billy snapped eleven photographs of the aerial events and recorded the sounds as it happened. The jet fighter left the area after its twenty-second unsuccessful attempt to pursue and contain the alien spacecraft.

"We extraterrestrial living forms have no authority yet to interfere by force with terrestrial concerns."

—**Ptaah**,
Pleiadian cosmonaut, 1975

April 14, 1976, 16:11 hours
One in a series of eleven photographs in which a Swiss Mirage fighter is seen attacking the Pleiadian spacecraft. The fighter has just completed a pass through the valley and is turning around to continue pursuit of the spacecraft. This photograph was taken just as the spacecraft reappeared at a low altitude above the valley floor in the midst of defensive maneuvers. These are the first photographs ever seen of such an aerial event, in which aerial combat between a fighter and a UFO was captured on film.

This series of photographs has been thoroughly analyzed by computers. A closer view appears in the computer photo analysis section of this book (see pages 58–59).

March 29, 1976, 18:10 hours
Two series of photographs were taken, one at 18:10 hours and the other at about 19:50 hours after a physical contact. Here, the craft approaches from the southwest and hovers before landing. The tree is fifty-two yards away. The craft is hovering beyond over a small valley.

"Throughout the investigation, I was impressed by Billy's courage. Even though he was being attacked, both mentally and physically by many, he was still willing to take us to the sites and reply to repeated questions with the same immutable answers."

—**Brit Elders**, investigator, 1978

"The first time I met Billy, I was extremely impressed by his openness, warmth, and sincerity. I particularly noticed his eyes when we first met and was awed by the fact that those eyes had perhaps seen more than any other living human being on this planet. But I was still dubious…until I began examining the contact sites with Stevens and Welch. You might say that this was my 'moment of truth'…especially the Hasenbol site…Once more I was impressed by the seemingly impossible task of faking a whole series (nine photos) of photographs such as were captured on film by Billy at this remote hilltop location."

—**Lee Elders**, investigator, 1978

March 29, 1976, 18:10 hours
Tree dimensions: thirty-one feet tall,
twenty-one feet diameter
Location: between Hasenbol and Langenberg

As the Meier experiences continued throughout March of 1976, a remarkable series of new photographs surfaced as the Pleiadians presented a new beamship and summoned Meier telepathically from Hinwel to a cold and windy mountain peak between Hasenbol and Langenberg to record the event on film. The footage is not only unique in composition but also offers a very difficult setting for manipulation and staging due to the cold, windy, and difficult terrain. The sequence series of nine incredible photographs show the beamship in flight. This image depicts the craft at the conclusion of the flight as it "parks" near a tree.

Two rolls of thirty-six prints were taken on March 29, 1976—unfortunately, today only nine frames remain; the others have disappeared along with hundreds of additional negatives through theft and manipulation by known and unknown sources.

"The culture shock one experiences between the initial psychological challenge and skepticism caused by claimed extraterrestrial contact and the actual hard-hitting reality of examining firsthand at least seven different correlating forms of evidence, which appear to be the result of visiting beings from another world, is staggering in consequence…particularly when this hard evidence cannot be easily dismissed by intelligent analysis when all the facts are taken into account."

—**Thom Welch**, investigator, 1978

March 29, 1976, 9:30 hours and 16:50 hours
Photographs on this page and the facing page show the Pleiadian cosmonaut's new variation type-3 spacecraft accompanied by two smaller, pilotless, remote-controlled ships that are limited to operation within a planet's atmosphere. The inset photograph above shows a small remote craft behind a tree branch on the upper right-hand side of the photograph on this page that wasn't found until the entire photograph was enlarged for detailed photo analyses. (In all of the photographs tested, the possibility of toss-in models, suspension lines or wires, photo trickery, mirror techniques, and paste-ups had been eliminated, as well as the many other methods of faking photographs, leaving the viewer to form their own opinion.)

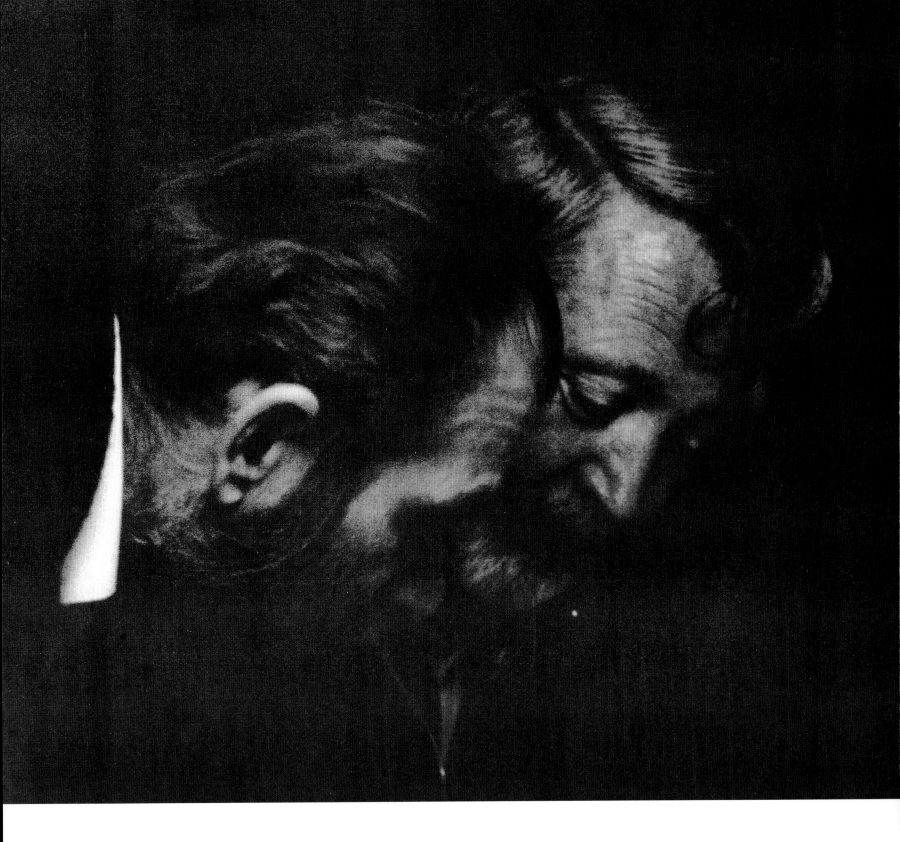

The Contactee: Eduard "Billy" Meier
Lee Elders took this photograph as Meier unveiled the metal samples of the
Pleiadian spacecraft for the first time.

Investigator: Col. Stevens
April 2,1978
Location: Hinterschmidruti, Switzerland

The Investigation

In August 1976, background events began to unfold in the form of a rather skeptical investigation into Billy Meier's unique and unprecedented experiences, initiated by experts in the field of UFO-related phenomena.

Meier heard a very unusual sound. A low, throbbing, humming sound that defied description. Then he saw it—a strange, silver disc-shaped craft circling slowly above. He couldn't believe his eyes!

The most experienced of the unsuspecting experts drawn to the Meier case was an enigma in his own right. He was an expert in the field of aircraft technology, and his participation in the peace negotiations in Tokyo six days prior to the end of World War II and the surrender of Japan, his later flights into and over communist China, and his consultations in the structural design of the Bolivian Air Force were remarkable stories in themselves. Historic events always appeared to be an integral part of Col. Stevens's life, as had been his in-depth investigation of the UFO phenomena around the world. Retired from the United States Air Force Air Technical Intelligence Center in 1963, the lieutenant colonel had since earned the reputation as being one of the top UFO investigators worldwide, a fact reflecting his successful scientific approach in hundreds of such cases. Little did he know that the Swiss case would prove to be his most exhausting and demanding challenge in his thirty years of UFO research and investigation.

In the fall of 1976, the evidence began to mount, pouring in at an alarming rate to Stevens's Arizona residence. Months before, he had received the first Meier photographs, courtesy of a cohort investigator in Europe. In the beginning, like everyone else who had come into contact with these precedent-setting photographs, he felt that they were too good; after all, no one had ever witnessed such quality in UFO photography before.

The accumulating evidence and information he had been receiving almost weekly finally spurred him into planning his first trip to the Swiss sites for the fall of 1977. Col. Stevens arrived in the most neutral country in the world, intent upon discovering the inside story behind the amazing claims. In addition to examining much of the evidence, he obtained statements from Mr. Meier as well as from many other witnesses and observed the daily activities of the Meier farmhouse firsthand. He was amazed by his observations—he felt something had happened there, something indefinable but stupendous, leaving forever its indelible mark of change. He had never before seen anything quite like it in his years of investigating other contactee cases.

Stevens saw the need for confidential security to protect the remains of Meier's hard evidence. It was a known fact that sometime between the fall of 1976 and the spring of 1977, a large amount of priceless data and materials had been

taken from Billy Meier. Magazine articles in France, Germany, Italy, and Switzerland had begun to appear in rapid succession, highlighting the Meier experience and releasing unauthorized photographs from the Meier collection. The premature release of the Meier contact case in Europe had brought many curious and sincere onlookers into the Meier farmhouse and had created a nightmare for Billy and his family. The unscrupulous were among those who found their way to the contactee, and they used every means available to "collect" negatives and rare film footage for "scientific testing" purposes. A trusting Billy had given some of them willingly for the benefit of analysis, since he was promised that they would be returned. Unfortunately, neither the materials nor the people who took them were ever seen again. In early 1978, it became apparent to Stevens that the theft and misuse of these unprecedented photographs and data were slowly reaching an alarming rate. Unless something was done quickly and confidentially, there would be little left for scientists to analyze, and the truth behind these events would be forever lost.

Upon his return, Col. Stevens needed to open a few doors. He contacted a close friend, Lee Elders, director of Intercep, whom he had been updating on new Meier information regularly. Intercep, a unique electronic counter-measure security firm, had a distinguished reputation for investigating and solving multinational clients' problems related to sophisticated corporate and industrial espionage—the theft of a firm's most prized possession: knowledge.

Intercep's focus on client confidentiality and in-depth investigation was most appealing to the captains of industry, for Intercep had been assigned to protect over $3 billion of sensitive client operations in their first two years in business. This was a highly impressive feat, but as were others, Stevens was most impressed by the behind-the-scenes activity that Intercep was noted for—in-depth investigation and research.

Lee Elders and his associates responded to their friend's request for help. Intercep accepted the role of safekeeping Meier's remaining evidence and expanding the investigation with the help of science. Such support offered a thorough opportunity to probe well beyond surface details and was the first time, in Stevens's recollection of thirty year tenure as a UFO investigator, that an "outside" professional investigative body had agreed to assist in a UFO investigation. In order to preserve the evidence for analysis and limit any prejudice or bias that could influence the judgment of scientists who would be involved in the testing

Location: Ober-Sadelegg
In this photograph, the beamship has moved further left, to the north, crossed a depression, and moved away along a stand of large pines to its right. The taller of those large pines to the right in the picture is two hundred yards away, and the far tree line is 350 yards away. The craft moved north to beyond the far tree line and then turned west and flew along that line to the end of those trees.

Photograph on this page:
Col. Stevens standing below area where the space-craft was photographed, for size comparison.

processes, Intercep initiated its first priorities, which included clamping a lid of secrecy on all activities surrounding the case.

In the weeks that followed, Thom Welch, Brit Elders, and a myriad of computer, laser, and photographic specialists were brought together by Stevens and Elders to conduct a most exhaustive and painstakingly detailed investigation. It became one of the most intense scientific probes ever undertaken in the history of the UFO contact phenomena. The remarkable photographs taken by Billy Meier were first on the list, and the lab facilities of selected specialists in various fields became the setting for a continuing step-by-step drama.

In early April of 1978, while science was at work, Stevens, the investigative team composed of Brit and Lee Elders, and Welch flew to Switzerland and the contact sites for new information and a more

August 1978
Location: Switzerland
Thom Welch stands on the exact site where two years earlier (March 29, 1976) photographs were taken (large photo left) before and after a contact took place with visitors from the Pleiades star system.

Witnesses

Col. Stevens and the investigative team were confronted with a substantial number of local witnesses who had personally observed remarkable events. Some even had photographed the Pleiadian spacecraft approaching and leaving the contact sites. Their phenomenal observations and experiences were further documented by many detailed interviews.

While testimony and depositions were taken, the investigative team went one step further to expose any potential embellishment or memorization in the witnesses' accounts. With the help of the psychology department of the University of Arizona, a precise list of questions was drawn up for the witnesses to answer. These answers were recorded for lie detection testing by special computers standing by in Northern California. Called a Psychological Stress Evaluation, these special computer voice analysis systems offered the most intricate, accurate, and sophisticated form of PSE and lie detection testing available.

The witnesses

The investigators: Lee Elders, Brit Elders, and Col. Stevens

Col. Stevens and Thom Welch interview Billy Meier.

The investigators interview the witnesses.

Photograph right:
The photographs in this book represent the better photographs taken from a specific series of photographs shot at different locations. The investigative team spent hours matching up the various series of photographs to create the accurate panorama of each experience, then cross-checked every detail for inconsistencies. Here we have two photographs taken at different times now matched together, displaying the broad panorama of a specific contact site.

The witnessed accounts were remarkably detailed and would demand a substantial imagination to create individually. But none of the investigators sensed any hint of deception. In fact, the sincerity felt from the witnesses as they answered the questions directly was disarming. It was no surprise that these witnesses passed the PSE tests with flying colors.

Of all the evidence of the ongoing events available for examination, the photographs seemed to re-create the events most vividly. In series—second by second—the photographs detailed the movements of the spacecraft in almost movie-like form during each event. The investigative team spent hours matching up these photographs to create the accurate panorama of each experience, then cross-checked every claimed detail for inconsistencies. In the hours of study and comparing notes, witness accounts, light and weather conditions, and various other factors, everything corresponded exactly, presenting one of the most detailed pictures imaginable of each event as it happened.

March 28, 1976, 16:50 hours
Location: Bachtelhornli-Unterbactel
A 3,000 percent blow-up of the craft in this photograph was made for analysis.
See pages 58–59 for the computer-analyzed images of this photograph.

"It is becoming increasingly difficult to remain objective in the face of the accumulating evidence, and we are impelled to a conclusion that the experience actually happened, that the disc-shaped craft photographed is really a UFO and that the case is legitimate. We are continuing the investigation into this on-going affair, and we intend to present the facts to the people, and we invite anyone to disprove them any way they can."

—**Col. Stevens**, 1978

Each form of evidence supporting Mr. Meier's experiences was impressive. To each of the investigators, one form of evidence or another usually stood out above the others in its impact. Each had different opinions and reasons why certain evidence was more supportive than others, but the fact that there were so many different types of evidence supporting the experiences—each difficult to dispute—along with the presence of hundreds of photographs in series, which were each startling in their own way, overwhelmed the team.

As they returned home with this amazing evidence intact, they focused on solving the difficulties inherent in finding unbiased scientists who would be willing to examine and study what was now in their possession. Security and confidentiality were essential if an accurate examination was to be made.

Each element of evidence had to be analyzed separately for its own merits or shortcomings, without the preliminary influence or prejudice that general knowledge of the Swiss events could cause. There was much to examine, and although the investigators would return to Switzerland again and again as new events developed, study and analysis of the incredible evidence and information they acquired became the top priority.

This series of photographs show Lee Elders and Col. Stevens comparing the actual site to the photographs taken by Billy Meier. Also shown are Billy Meier and his youngest son aiding the process.

Computer and Laser Photo Examination

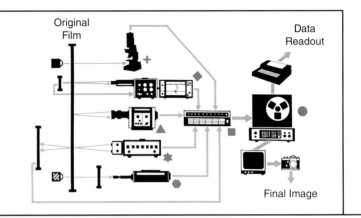

Because of the incredible nature of the Meier photographs, an exhaustive series of photogrammetric tests was designed by consultants hired by the investigative team whose specialties centered on optical engineering, special effects, computer analyses, and laser-scanning techniques. The objective was to analyze these photographs more thoroughly than any other UFO-type photographs had ever been analyzed before, utilizing additional, highly advanced procedures and technology drawn from sophisticated aerospace and nuclear medicine applications.

Using the most advanced graphics computer systems and electronic equipment available, the specialists began testing for trick photography, models, strings, and special dark room techniques. Applying electron microscopes, laser scanning, and computer functions, the film grain itself was examined for any distortion resulting from double exposure, lamination, or projection methods. The testing became intense, with three photographs (from the fighter sequence taken April 14, 1976 on pages 38–39, from the valley sequence taken March 29, 1976 on pages 42–43, and one from the log-pile sequence taken March 8, 1975, seen on page 29) drawing the center of attention. For consistent comparison, photographs showing variation type-4 craft were focused upon (type-4 craft from fighter sequence, April 14, 1976, and from valley sequence, March 28, 1976, seen here).

Further testing targeted on lighting angles, shadows, and edge focus of all objects in each photograph searching

Computer Functions
1. **Histogram**: defines light intensity values, Z scale
2. **Edge Identification**: clearly shows all lines (edges) in pictures
3. **Edge Enhancement**: improves visual quality of edges in pictures
4. **Spatial Filtering**: separates different light values (frequency)
5. **Contour Identification**: topographic (3-D) map of object
6. **Focus Index**: identifies edges as function of distance
7. **Contrast Enhancement**: improves visual quality of hazy picture
8. **Image Enhancement**: improves edges and finer details of object
9. **Geometry Function**: calculates size, distance, aspect ratio of objects

Laboratory Equipment
+ Electron Microscope: powerful close-up microscope
♦ Microdensitometer: measures density of film grain
∗ Interferometer: measures waveform/frequency of film crystals (as lenses)
● Infraredometer: measures infrared light not visible to naked eye
▲ Vidicon Tube: converts picture to electronic image
■ Digitizer: converts vidicon image to 300,000 computer cells called pixels
● Image Process Computer: defines, analyzes, measures elements of photo

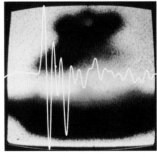
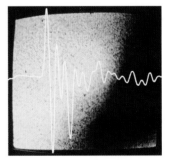

Film grain analysis by laser-scanning microdensitometer shows consistent homogeneous patterns, no overlapping film grains; eliminates overlays, multiple exposures, multiple printings, and darkroom techniques.
+ ♦ 1.

3,000 percent blow-up of type-4 craft from original picture; note ornamental-looking protrusions; rim of craft appears to be moving.

✛ ◆ ▲ ■ 1. 3. 7. 8.

Thermogram—color density separations—low frequencies. Properties of light/time of day are correct; light values on ground are reflected in craft bottom; eliminates double exposure and paste-ups.

◆ ■ ● 1. 4.

Thermogram—color density separations—high frequencies. Properties of light/time of day are correct; light values on ground are reflected in craft bottom; eliminates double exposure and paste-ups.

◆ ■ ● 1. 4.

One in a series of eleven photographs in which a Swiss Mirage fighter is seen attacking the Pleiadian spacecraft.

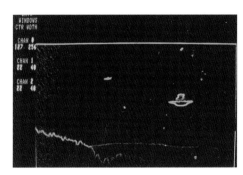

Edge identification on fighter attack photograph—eliminates strings, wires, paste-ups, small models; defines edges for distance/focus and craft/object size calculations, solid object.

◆ ▲ ■ 1. 2. 6. 9.

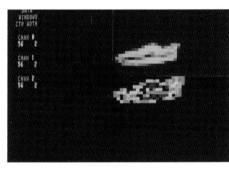

Edge identification of jet—eliminates strings, wires, paste-ups, small models due to computer size/distance calculations. Density average—object is 3-dimensional due to variable colors.

✛ ◆ ▲ ■ 1. 2. 4. 6. 9.

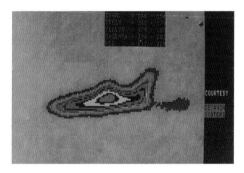

Z-scale contour of infrared copy print with band pass filtering—topographical view based upon illumination; blue is profile edge of wing closest to camera; shows rear edge (red) slightly larger than front edge due to blur factor, proving movement of jet; jet exhaust visible, amplified by infrared.

✛ ◆ ▲ ■ 1. 4. 5.

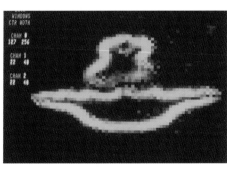

Edge identification of spacecraft—eliminates strings, wires, paste-ups, small models due to computer size/distance calculations. If a string or wire support were present, they would be visible in this test photo.

✛ ◆ ▲ ■ 1. 2. 3. 6.

Density average—object is three-dimensional due to variable colors.

✛ ▲ ■ 1. 3. 4.

Z-scale contour of infrared copy print with band pass filtering—topographical view based upon illumination; shows supernormal light distortion properties—note purple field flowing into or coming off of craft edge. No combustion engine exhaust visible.

✛ ◆ ▲ ■ 1. 4. 5.

for paste-ups, overlays, and other forms of fakery as well as data for calculations of the size and distance away of each object. The computers would indicate any inconsistency, in addition to providing a three-dimensional, topographical view of the objects in question. Image enhancement and edge enhancement were done to improve the qualities of the picture to reveal any suspicious lines, wires, or other aspects that would throw the photographs under doubt. Even more tests were employed to detect other-than-visible-spectrum light or energy captured within the film crystals.

Additional, more-evolved testing and study of the photographs actively continues today, but as seen here in photographs of some of the tests, and as noted in the conclusions, everyone was in for a surprise.

Photogrammetric Analysis Conclusions

The film was examined microscopically and processed by a laser-scanning microdensitometer. Analyses of the film grain (density contour plots) showed no overlapping film crystals, eliminating the possibility of darkroom techniques or film overlays and indicating a consistent, homogeneous grain pattern normally expected of an authentic photograph.

The negatives, transparencies, prints, and color separations were carefully examined for photo paste-up, models at short range, suspended on a string or tossed/propelled into the field of view, and improper focus, distance, or size relationships. Edge enhancement proved that there is no string, filament, or other support holding the craft. Close-up examination of the craft edges and those of other reference objects in the photographs always showed that the focus, distance, and size relationships are proper, eliminating the possibility of small models at short range and paste-up techniques.

Examination of the location of the shadows and highlights in the photographs verifies that the craft and surrounding landscape were shot under precisely the same conditions of light. The craft was noted to have an extremely smooth, reflective metallic surface, and the light values of the landscape were reflected in the bottom of the craft.

August 3, 1975, 17:20 hours • Distance to log pile: 198 yards • Distance to tree line: 280 yards • Location: Ober-Sadelegg
One of the first photographs analyzed by computer photogrammetric methods. Nothing was found to indicate a hoax. An entire series of photographs was shot here as the craft continued to move toward the photographer and to the left over the trees out of the picture.

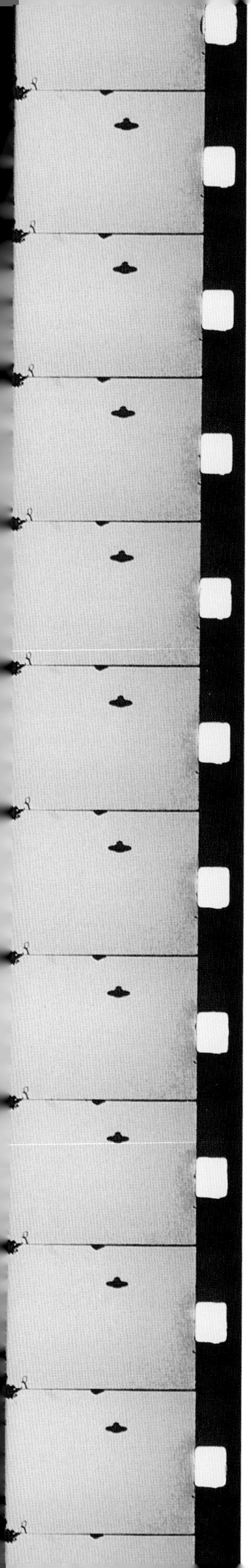

Additionally, Z-scale contour and Z-scale density average tests confirmed the craft to be a large, three-dimensional object.

In short, nothing was found to indicate trick photography, models, or other suspicious techniques. Nothing was found to indicate a hoax. Distance and size measurements are proper in relation to location measurements taken by the investigators, and the reported size of the craft is appropriate to the calculations done by the computers.

While this surprised many of the specialists who were expecting to find the string, or some other "technique," more was to come. While experimenting with special emission scanning techniques, unusual "energy" fields were found in a photograph surrounding only the area of the craft. The light frequencies of these fields were above the visible spectrum and remained in the photograph after the visible spectrum of light had been cancelled out. Under further analysis another test revealed supernormal light distortion properties around the craft in a photograph under certain ranges of the light spectrum.

Such things have never been found before, and while they do not affect the validity of the photographs, such findings excited the desire to learn more through further advanced testing and study of these photographs. Interestingly, the majority of specialists involved were unaware of the other forms of evidence supporting Billy Meier's experiences when these preliminary tests supported the validity of the photographs.

8mm Movie Footage

During his many meetings with the Pleiadians, Billy had the opportunity to film seven different segments of 8mm movie footage. This footage is one of the most precedent-setting forms of evidence supporting his experiences.

Taken during various seasons over the years, these exciting segments were acquired for the most part by automatic operation of the camera after Meier had set it up on its tripod, not an easy feat since he was handicapped with the loss of his left arm in a 1963 bus accident in Turkey. Although the automatic operation of the camera alleviated the obvious problems he faced, it also served a far more important purpose, for it allowed the photographer and the Pleiadian spacecraft the opportunity to appear simultaneously in one of the segments. This also left Meier free to take still pictures (as seen here) of the scene as Semjase's spacecraft approached.

The first of seven segments of film taken during the first year of the events shows the earlier

(1975, variation type-2) craft of Semjase's hovering, then circling a tree several times before moving off. Incredibly, the treetop is seen to move violently from the force of the craft as it passes over. In the second segment, cars moving along the road in both directions are plainly visible behind and below the hovering spacecraft. And during the third segment of film, the craft literally disappears at one point then reappears after a short time. Examination of this film portion shows that no tampering with or splicing of the film is apparent.

All of the footage is just as remarkable. As of 1978, less than a dozen movie segments of UFO-type craft have been seen by the general public. Such movie footage is considered quite rare. By comparison, these seven stunning segments of movie film are providing a wealth of evidence for examination in connection with the results of the on-site investigations.

This scanning electron microscope photograph at 2,000 diameters shows the remarkably efficient conductivity in this metallic specimen. This photograph was made without the gold foil covering ordinarily needed for improved conductivity to prevent electron fogging of the image. Because of the unprecedented high conductivity of the metal specimen itself, we are able to clearly view not only the crystals but even the X-ray images of other faces of these crystals in this specimen.

Metal Samples Analysis

"The next morning we checked on Meier physically to see if he was up and around. We were told that he was still sleeping and that he had a contact during the night (his 105th), and that he had a surprise for us. We couldn't wait to get up the hill to see what happened....Finally, at the end of the day when everyone had left, Meier said, 'I have a surprise for you.' He then produced a small package of amber crystals that he said, 'Quetzal had delivered for us.' The package also contained four metal pieces, one biological sample, and nine mineral and crystal specimens for us to have analyzed."

—**Col. Stevens**, 1978

This photograph exhibits an area of a metal specimen enlarged to 500 diameters. Evidence of what looks like mechanical manipulation to an extremely fine degree was found. Notice the discreet marks in a diagonal direction bordered by an area that looks as if it has been plowed.

Upon their return home, the investigators provided scientists with a small specimen of one of four states of space-craft metal for confidential study and analysis. At first, broader scope metallurgical analyses were accomplished, and then more in-depth, highly sophisticated examination began. These detailed analyses continue today. However, from the beginning, unique qualities in the metal samples were detected, causing the scientists involved to note that they had never seen anything like it before.

Preliminary analyses revealed unique properties, rare transition elements, and an unusually high level of purity in the state of the metal that, in reference to our present technology, was not immediately explainable. The metal specimen's general characteristics seemed to indicate a non-electrolytic, cold fusion synthesis process not generally known to Earth technology.

Landing Tracks

The more than 130 meetings with the Pleiadian cosmonauts have taken place in various moist, grassy meadows that dot the forested Swiss countryside in the Canton Zurich region. Consequently, a substantial number of physical traces remain of these events, including burned bushes, broken branches and twigs, trails of identifiable footprints, and most uniquely, landing tracks left by the various extraterrestrial spacecraft. The majority of these landing marks present an intriguing form of evidence in the fact that, even seasons later, they could still be seen.

Semjase's seven-meter ships (twenty-one feet diameter), types 1 through 4, land on tripod legs that are extended from the lower surface of the craft. These legs have circular dish-shaped shoes that leave a round, swirled-down pattern in the grass. The grass is swirled-down in a counter-clockwise direction and does not rise again. Although new grass does grow up in the swirled-down area, the new grass does not grow in the same manner as that of the surrounding grass. In the print areas left by the landing gear of these spacecraft, the new grass is not as lush and does not grow as tall or as dense as the rest of the grass in the surrounding meadow, leaving traces that are visible many months later.

The pilotless, remote-controlled spacecraft seen accompanying Semjase's seven-meter craft on several occasions are approximately three and a half or five meters in diameter and land on the three hemispherical structures spaced 120 degrees apart on their undersides. When landed, they do not rest heavily on these round protrusions, but they also leave the grass and vegetation below them swirled down in a counter-clockwise direction. The same unusual growth characteristics of new grass appearing in the landing tracks occur as well.

To the experts, these tracks represent a curious phenomenon not easily duplicated or explained, especially when considering the remote terrain of some of the landing sites. Scores of these landing tracks were photographed by witnesses when they were fresh, and later at various times during the changing seasons, creating a record for study through time-lapse photography. They represent another form of evidence supporting the physical level of Mr. Meier's experiences—remaining physical traces that might be expected of such unworldly physical events.

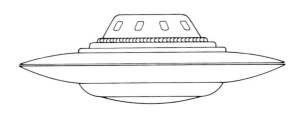

Variation Type-1 Craft
Seven-Meter Reconnaissance Ship
(21 feet diameter) carries crew of three and has
interplanetary capability of travel. Claimed to
be several hundred years old and was replaced
because of radiation leakage problem.

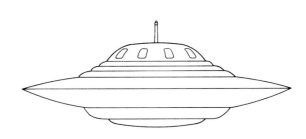

Variation Type-2 Craft
Seven-Meter Reconnaissance Ship
(21 feet diameter) carries crew of three and has
interplanetary capability of travel.

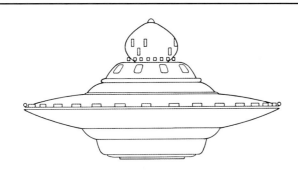

Variation Type-3 Craft
Seven-Meter Reconnaissance Ship
(21 feet diameter) carries crew of three and has
interplanetary capability of travel.

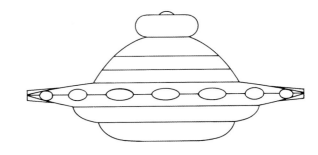

Variation Type-4 Craft
Seven-Meter Reconnaissance Ship
(21 feet diameter) carries crew of three, has time
travel capability and interplanetary capability
of travel.

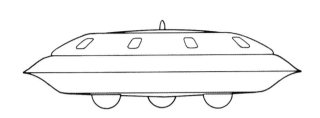

Variation Type-5 Craft
Telemeter Disc for Reconnaissance
Remote-controlled, three-and-one-half and
five-meter versions, place for one, travel limited
to planetary atmosphere.

"If a spaceship breaks through the barrier of light velocity without reaching hyper-space instantly, a catastrophe is due for ship and crew."

—**Semjase**, Pleiadian cosmonaut, 1976

"A spacecraft has to be equipped with two different propulsion systems, one for the normal propulsion and another one for the hyper-space propulsion method. It is only when time and space have ceased to exist that we are capable of traveling through light years of distance in a matter of seconds."

—**Semjase**, Pleiadian cosmonaut, 1975

"Our spaceships are protected by a screen of energy which automatically rejects any kind of resistance and every bit of matter. This protective screen is, in fact, identical with the specific gravitational field which we build up around our ships. With this protective screen we are able to neutralize the gravitational field effect of any planet we want to approach."

—**Semjase**, Pleiadian cosmonaut, 1976

Spacecraft (Photographed)

During the years, a number of different types of Pleiadian spacecraft have been seen in connection with these remarkable experiences. Each has been photographed at one time or another and appears among the numerous photographs associated with the witnessed events. Each craft has a different purpose or represents a "newer, more modern version," according to the extraterrestrial visitors. Semjase's use of a new or different craft was always the subject of obvious questions from Mr. Meier, and in explanation, the Pleiadian cosmonaut related some of the basic details about their reconnaissance ships, particularly those of the class-type used most often when contact activities with residents of a planet took place.

The visitors from the Pleiades have many different types or classes of spacecraft, some of which are capable of interplanetary and interdimensional space travel. Most of the Pleiades spacecraft operating around Earth belong to a specific category of small reconnaissance ships with interplanetary capabilities. From five to twenty-two and a half meters (seventeen to seventy-six feet) in diameter, they are able to fly from planet to planet, if desired, but also operate within the planetary atmospheres. They provide room for one to seven beings, depending upon their size. The various craft used most frequently by Semjase and her crew are reconnaissance ships approximately seven meters in diameter, having just enough room for a crew of three.

Among their technical equipment aboard is a device for dimensional and hyperdimensional transitions (jumps) that transport the ship and crew in a twinkling of an eye through uncounted light years of distance, as we understand it. These crafts are equipped with an additional propulsion system allowing slower travel at speeds below the speed of light in physical dimensions, as well as artificial gravitation and artificial environment systems for comfort and ease of travel.

Another type of craft, seen with the seven-meter reconnaissance ships, is the remote-controlled Telemeter Disc, varying in size from three to five meters in diameter. This class of scout ship is used to gather data and monitor, providing information to the "mother ship" controlling each disc or storing information for retrieval at a later date. Equipped with extensive sensing devices, the larger versions also have space aboard for one occupant as a passenger or pilot.

The Pleiadian Connection

"We, too, are still far removed from perfection and have to evolve constantly, just like yourselves. We are neither superior nor superhuman, nor are we missionaries....We feel duty bound to the citizens of Earth, because our forefathers were your forefathers..."

—**Semjase**, Pleiadian cosmonaut, February 8, 1975

The Great Pyramid of Cheops, Egypt

Egypt

This statement by the cosmonaut Semjase stimulated the Intercep investigators. Could there be an historical tie between Earth and the Pleiades, and if so, were there recorded accounts of other "Billy Meiers" that might be found in the written and oral histories of ages past? The research began, and soon came the surprises.

The Elderses and Thom Welch began to experience the sensations Schliemann must have felt when he unearthed the legendary city of Troy, succeeding because he had dared believe in and follow the mythology of Homer's *Iliad*. It has been proven in the past when dealing with large gaps of time in history that, on many occasions, the truth becomes transposed into legend. Such became the challenge of this team, and after only a few weeks, a wealth of history began to reveal itself under a new light. The first doors to open for the investigators were over forty-five centuries old.

From ancient manuscripts and cuneiforms to legends and mythology, no stars are more talked about than the Pleiades, nor are any other stars considered more influential to humankind's destiny. From the time of Egyptian Pharaoh Ahmose I at the time of King David of Judea, numerous cuneiform tablets were addressed to the Pleiades, expressing a budding civilization's thoughts to its mentors. Egypt provided only a small part of the almost magical love and respect our world has shed on the Pleiadian constellation and its visiting inhabitants. With November, the "Pleiade-month," early peoples began their year, and on the day of these stars' midnight culmination, November 17, no petition was ever presented in vain to the ancient Kings of Persia.

The Temple of Hathor

In the old spiritual city of Denderah, beside the Nile River, lies the Temple of Hathor that is dedicated to the Goddess of Love and the Stars of Hathor—the Pleiades. In this temple a marvel of man's beginning can be found: an eons-old carving on the ceiling, intricate in design. A star clock, first carved in early BCE, celebrates the Pleiades, marking the greater center on which our solar system revolves, taking 25,827.5 years to complete one cycle. This correlates with other similar stone carvings half a world away such as the celebrated Mayan calendar and that of the Hopi, which are based on the same cycle of the Pleiades. These clocks have survived the ages and are still accurate to a high degree.

> "The pagan Arabs, according to Hafiz, fixed here (The Pleiades) the seat of immortality, as did the Berbers, or Kabyles, of Northern Africa, and widely separated from them, the Dyaks of Borneo; all thinking them to be the central point of the Universe."
>
> —**Richard H. Allen**, *Star Names: Their Lore and Their Meanings*

The Great Pyramid of Cheops

The Great Pyramid was riddled with Pleiadian mystery. Its seven mystical chambers, suggested Professor Charles Piazzi, commemorate the seven visible stars of the Pleiades, for some unknown but important reason. Amazingly, the

In describing a great Inca temple in Peru, Garcilaso de la Vega in his *The Incas*, pages 71 to 116, stated, "The room nearest that of the Moon was devoted to Venus, to the Pleiades and to all the other stars. Venus was honored as the sun's page, who accompanies him on his way, now following him, now preceding him. The Indians considered the other stars as servants of the Moon, and this was why they were represented near her. The constellation of the Pleiades was particularly revered."

The residents of South America were not alone. Even though the Pleiades were honored everywhere in ancient Peru as the arbiters of human destiny, we find that the Seven Sisters are also revered in the Caribbean islands. The Pleiades are considered the location of the Creator of the Universe, where God lives, the exact center of heaven, and the location of God's house by the Cunas, as well as by other tribes scattered throughout this part of our world.

The Cunas say that the Pleiades are the soul of God:

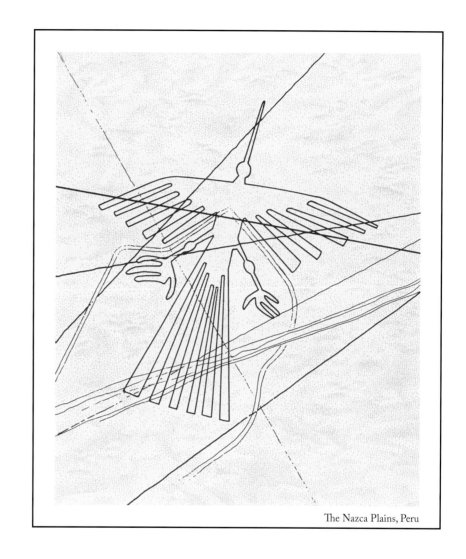

The Nazca Plains, Peru

It seems as though there is a constant struggle going on in the sky between the people of light and goodness, and the people of darkness and evil. Ikwaniktipippi, in describing certain celestial bodies, referred to this battle. He spoke of the Pleiades as seven heros who are arrowmakers who prepare fiery shafts for the battle. At other times, the Pleiades are the soul of God or where God lives…*

---

* Clyde Keeler, *Secrets of the Cuna Earthmother* (New York: Exposition Press, 1960), 84.

"The Calina Carib myth runs more or less as follows: The universe has its source in Amana, a virgin mother and water goddess who has no navel (i.e. was never born), a beautiful woman whose body ends in a serpent. She is the essence of time, has borne all things, can adopt any shape, dwells in the waters of the heavens and exercises her power from the Pleiades."

—**Walter Krickenberg**, *Pre-Columbian American Religions*, 1968

"The Pleiades was the constellation in the night sky most in the minds of the Incas and foremost in their stellar Pantheon. It was called Capac Collea Coyllur, 'The Star of the Overflowing Grain Bins,' and possessed the Power of Bringing Things into Being."

—**Walter Krickenberg**, *Pre-Columbian American Religions*, 1968

In the book *Pathways to the Gods: The Mystery of the Andes Lines*, we find on pages 58–59 a map of the Nazca Valley floor showing many of the long lines that run for miles over broken terrain in perfectly straight formation. Tony Morrison, the author, calls the great rectangle, beginning with the tail of the figure of the Thunderbird, The Plaza of the Pleiades, because it is oriented directly to the rising of the Pleiades at the estimated time of construction. Other lines are oriented to the setting of the Pleiades.

"An archeological bronze medallion in the museum of Heraklion in Greece, called 'The Disc of Phaistos' (17th Century BCE), shows, engraved in relief, in spiral form, from the center out, a story of a celestial visitation by beings who arrived in a disc-shaped craft from the sky. The seven dots enclosed in a circle that is repeated many times is believed to represent the Pleiades."

—**Col. Stevens**, 1978

"The seven-dot single quote symbol, according to this theory, can hardly represent anything other than the cluster of the Pleiades."

—**Robert Burnham Jr.**, *Burnham's Celestial Handbook*

The Disc of Phaistos
Note saucer-type figure above, third row down from the top edge.

Volume II

"In the past we have witnessed those who were unable to determine the truth or were frightened when confronted with it; this serves no purpose for terrestrial man or ourselves. The fear should never be present as all men hold the truth within themselves and must only know this to find it."

—**Semjase**, Pleiadian cosmonaut, 1976

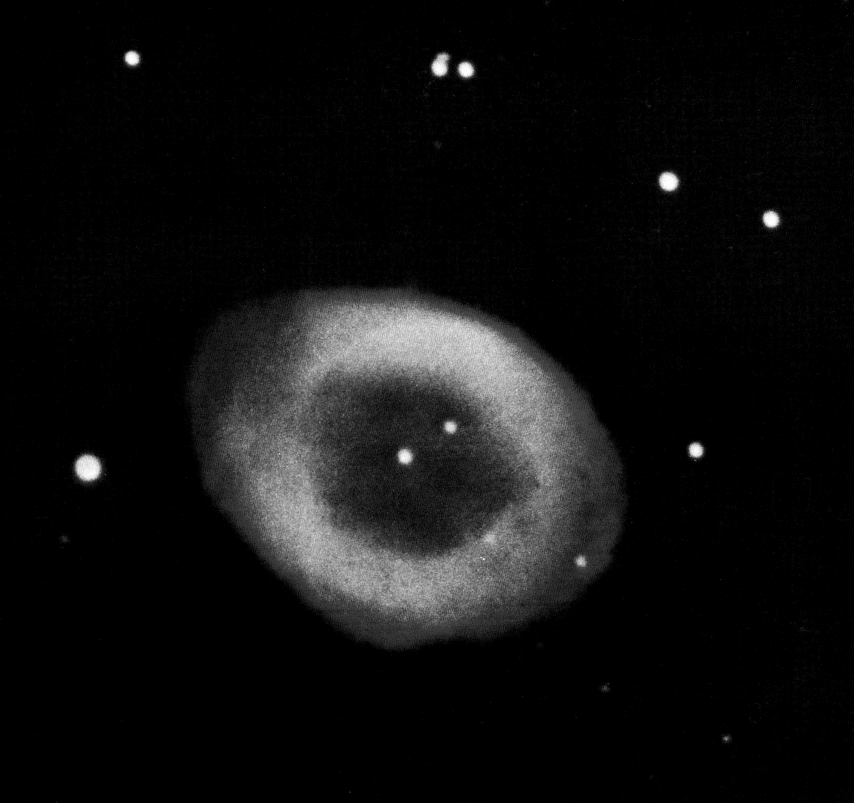

The Ring Nebula of Lyra
The Pleiadians refer to this as "The Eye of God."

The Great Orion Nebula

"Life on Earth may have started when spacemen landed here billions of years ago."

—**Professor Thomas Gold**, Cornell University

"All this visible universe is not unique in nature and we must believe that there are, in other regions of space, other beings and other men."

—**Lucretius**, 99–55 BCE

"I do not doubt for an instant that in our galaxy and in all the countless host of others there must be many civilizations, most of which are technically and intellectually far in advance of us poor mortals on this little planet of a very average and undistinguished star."

—**John Macvey**, astronomer

"UFOs really exist and apparently come from other planets."

—**Javier Garzon**, astronomer

"The UFO phenomenon is a challenge to mankind. It is the duty of scientists to take up this challenge, to disclose the nature of the UFO, and to establish the scientific truth."

—**Dr. Felix Zigel**, Soviet researcher

"The signs are increasing. The lights in the sky will appear red, blue, green, rapidly. They will grow. Someone is coming from very far and wants to meet the people of the Earth. Meetings have already taken place. But those who have really seen have been silent."

—*The Prophies of Pope John XXIII*, Pier Carpi, 1935

"Listen to your inner selves and look into the infinity of space and time. There reverberate the song of the stars and the harmony of the spheres.

"Each sun is a thought of Creation, each planet a mode of that thought. In order that you may know divine thought, O souls, you painfully descend along the paths of the seven planets and their seven heavens and ascend once again.

"What do the stars do? What do the numbers say? What do the spheres revolve? O souls that are lost and saved, they relate, they sing, they revolve your destinies."

—Édouard Schuré, *The Great Initiates:*
A Fragment from Hermes, 1912

The Pleiades

The Pleiades

"Many a night I saw the Pleiads, rising thro' the mellow shade,
Glitter like a swarm of fire-flies tangled in a silver braid."
—Lord Alfred Tennyson

The Seven Sisters, a cluster of stars, have guided people, far removed from each other, in agriculture and commercial affairs simply by rising and setting. Their twinkling brilliance has been the source of wishful admiration and critical observation on every continent, in every age. They have been worshipped by some, celebrated by others, and recognized for their beauty and "sweet influence" by most.

"Men mark their rising with the solar rays,
The harbinger of summer's brighter days."
—Aratus of Soli, poet

Most commonly referred to in today's text by their ancient Greek name, Pleiades (Plee ´ya dēz), these suns carry names from all areas of history. The Romans called them the Virgins of Spring, the Australians labeled them the Young Girls, and many civilizations denoted them as the Seven Doves. The Hindus pictured them as the Flame, typical of the god Agni, who represented the source of fire, and the Bible refers to them as the Seven Stars or the Pleiades.

"Canst thou bind the sweet influences of the Pleiades or loose the bands of Orion?"
—Job 38:31

"Seek him that maketh the seven stars and Orion, and turneth the shadow of death into morning, and maketh day dark with night: that calleth for the waters of the sea, and poureth them out upon the face of the earth: The Lord is his name."
—Amos 5:8

Possibly one of the most carefully studied regions of the firmament, the Seven Sisters are located in the constellation of Taurus, the Bull. Clearly visible in the northern hemisphere on a winter night, they resemble a tiny reproduction of the Little Dipper and are often mislabeled as such.

These sparkling orbs have fascinated minds for centuries, and in the eighteenth century a comet hunter, Charles Messier, was the first to chart and identify them. The primitive equipment of the day often allowed amateur astronomers to mistakenly label stationary objects as comets, so, to assist his fellow celestial gazers, Messier worked diligently from his observation atop the Hotel de Cluny in Paris. In 1771 he published his first catalogue of forty-five non-cometary objects, and it was in this register that the Pleiades were designated M45.

Several astronomers have charted many suns in the area of M45. Today we know that of the several thousand which appear in this tiny sector, 250 are recognized as members of this galactic cluster; the rest lie in the depths of space beyond the system. Once all of the fainter stars have been more carefully examined, the total may rise to a figure closer to 500.

The unique celestial showpiece is easily tracked by first locating the giant red star of Betelguese, which appears in the Orion constellation as the shoulder of the Great Hunter. Next finding Aldebaran, a first-magnitude star in Taurus, draw an imaginary line between the two. Extend the line in a northwest direction almost an equal distance past Aldebaran. Here it will terminate just south of the beautiful Seven Stars.

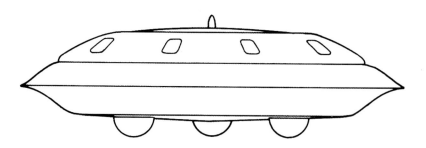

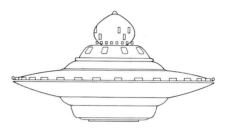

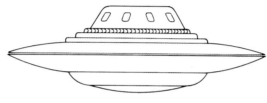

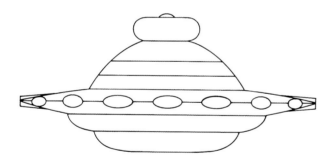

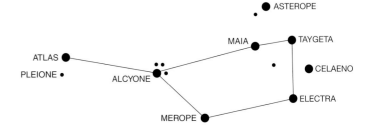

A tightly grouped cluster of suns in our own galaxy, six of the seven are generally discernible by the unaided eye, Alcyone being the brightest. It has a magnitude of 2.9 and is classified as a B5, blue-white star whose primary element is helium with an approximate temperature of 13,000 degrees Celsius. The magnitude of these luminous orbs range from the meek twinkling of Sterope (or Asterope), which is also blue-white but is type B8 with an apparent magnitude of 5.8, to the brilliance of Alcyone, which is thought by some to exceed our sun's refulgence one thousand times. As difficult as it may be for our minds to fathom, this light, which we categorize, classify, and gaze into the heavens to search out, has been traveling toward us for a century and a half before we perceive it!

Cave paintings, hieroglyphics, legends, mythology, and written languages have depicted these shimmering beams as a positive force throughout civilization's history. Their position in the expanse of darkened heavens throughout key times in the calendar year does not fully account for the remarkable influence attributed to them.

> "For see! the gathering flocks to shelter tend,
> And from the Pleiads fruitful show'rs descend."
> —**Alexander Pope**, poet

> "When the constellations were first designed, the Pleiades rose heliacally at the beginning
> of April, and were the sign of the return of spring."
> —**E. Walter Maunder**, astronomer

The mysterious beauty and peaceful connotations are referred to in text, both past and present, as the Seven Stars, yet one of them is not visually seen. Almost a universal tradition suggests that one of them has been misplaced or is hidden and so was deemed the "Lost Pleiad" by the Greeks. Possibly, sometime in the distant past, one of these stars was much brighter than it appears now. It is a known fact that stars vary in brilliance, and one of the Pleiades, mythology is uncertain as to which, may have lost its gleam during some far remote time. However, there is not a definitive explanation for the repeated description of seven, and it seems quite amazing that all cultures of antiquity were aware of the seventh star, which is masked from the view of the inhabitants of Earth.

> "As seven, their fame is on the tongues of men,
> Though six alone are beaming on the eye."
> —**Aratus of Soli**, poet

The Experience Continues

The beamship arrived soon after Billy had stopped his moped in a small clearing, and once again it was Semjase who emerged. He noted how her petite frame moved with an air of relaxed grace. Blond, shoulder-length hair framed well-defined facial features that were accented by almond-shaped, wide-set eyes of a pale blue color. The irises seemed elongated. When he extended his hand in greeting, a specific variance in their physical characteristics caught his attention. Her hand was small and delicate with the same number of digits as his, but her fingers moved with greater flexibility and showed no sign of an upper joint. When she brushed the hair from her flawless complexion, Meier's eyes widened once more—Semjase's ears were quite unusual, being smaller and set higher on the head, and were without lobes but instead continued in a straight line until they smoothed into her jaw. His quizzical look was answered with a laugh from the cosmonaut who asked if he expected all creatures in the universe to be identical when duplicated structures cannot be found on one small planet, Earth.

The first sixty-eight contacts were between Semjase, the Pleiadian, and Eduard "Billy" Meier, a simple earthy farmer and caretaker who loves the land and the beauty of nature. Headstrong and determined yet concerned for the welfare of others, Billy is not that different from most people; so why was he allowed to meet the visitors from a distant star? He had been receptive to the cooling sensations across his forehead and the unheard voice that led him through the dense forest of his native Switzerland to the unworldly meetings. The open attitude, however, was only a small part in the Pleiadians' reasoning of selection.

"If we decide to come in contact with an Earth-human, and the contact is to be continued for a long period of time, we must first study that individual for a full decade. This is done for the safety of all concerned, as he must be able to recognize the truth, for the truth shall give him the necessary balance in his attitudes."
—**Semjase**, Pleiadian cosmonaut, 1975

Telepathic communication preceded all face-to-face meetings, but Semjase assured him that unless his thoughts were focused on the Pleiadians or his mind was completely clear, they were forbidden to penetrate his thoughts, even through the use of this invisible mode of contact. To do so would be to violate two highly regarded principles: privacy and free will. Both are considered important to the development of an individual or society and terrestrial man must be allowed to make conscious decisions and then learn to be responsible for what he has created.

March 29, 1976, 19:50 hours
Location:Hasenbol-Langenberg
The dark spot in the haze moved southeast toward the camera, and Meier began filming (page 96). Setting the shot up with the handle bars of his moped, he continued to capture the movement of the beamship across the horizon (seen here and page 101).

"For the present, the Earth-human holds the weight of his destiny on his own shoulders. However, should a time arise where we would find it necessary to involve ourselves in certain matters pertaining to Earth, it would be done to prevent an aberration or possible cataclysm, that would affect the depths of cosmic space beyond the conscious thoughts of the Earth-human."

—**Semjase**, Pleiadian cosmonaut, 1976

"Thought transmission is the purest form of communication, as the conversation may not be manipulated into something it is not."

—**Ptaah**, Pleiadian cosmonaut, 1975

The unearthly meetings had graced the Swiss countryside in a myriad of locations during the first year of contact. Semjase had introduced Meier to two other cosmonauts, both male, who also had duties pertaining to this sector of the heavens. Ptaah, who Billy described as an elderly gentleman with compassionate wisdom, was generally stationed on the completely self-sufficient mother ship. Quetzal (Ket-´säl), the base commander, reminded Billy of a studious businessman. Each of them would exchange minimal dialogue with the farmer, while the majority of contacts would continue with Semjase.

The physical meetings with the returning spacecraft and its occupants were now occurring on a regular basis. With each new encounter, a stronger friendship and understanding developed, which permitted Meier the opportunity to enter into bolder questioning, such as, "why was there not a mass appearance to the general public?" He was surprised by the defiant, yet well-defined, response.

Vast publicity was not in the spectrum of their tasks for many reasons, the primary being the initial reaction of the "Earth-human," which was very unpredictable. True, there would be many who would be open to the thought of life existing on other worlds, but there would be countless numbers who would "fall into complete hysteria and become ill of spirit." Some of those who accepted the reality of other life would look to the visitors for miraculous cures for the ills of the Earth that mankind have created. Also, there would probably be a few who would try to take possession of the beamship to use for control and power over the rest of the population. A craft, which is so scientifically advanced, could be devastating if commanded by those who were "impure of thought."

Understanding this expressed logic of the crew in their determination not to land in a major metropolis, the farmer was still plagued by a question: "Am I the only one?"

In response, he was told that one who remained solely in the material sphere of greed and ego would never be permitted in such a meeting nor would any purpose be served if the visitors were to present themselves to a person who was afraid of them or of personal harm or ridicule that may be directed toward them due to the contacts. Only those who maintained a delicate balance and had demonstrated that absolute trust and confidence could be placed at their disposal were selected for the unique encounters.

"In the course of our duties, we do, here and there, approach the denizens of various worlds, select some individuals, and communicate with them. This we do only when a race is in a higher stage of evolution. Then we explain to them that they are not the only thinking beings in the universe."

—**Semjase**, Pleiadian cosmonaut, 1975

He knew her words often seemed strangely harsh, but he understood that they were not designed as a method of attack but only as a gentle scolding based on past experiences with similar situations. He realized that if the Pleiadians could find their way through diverse obstacles, the people of Earth could as well, if they so desired. It was times like this that made it difficult for Meier to return to the routines that his life demanded, because he often discovered that he was positioned in the middle of his own mixed emotions.

When asked if a friend could accompany the farmer to one of the contacts, the Pleiadians explained that should they allow him to bring an interested party, for any reason, a chain reaction would be set in motion, for there would be no reason to refuse anyone else. Thus, the friend who had joined Meier may have a friend, who may have a friend, and so on, until all time was spent conversing. Should they allow this ongoing cycle to begin, there would be no reason to be selective of individuals.

A few months passed before Meier again broached the subject, this time suggesting that an additional person involved in the meetings would serve as stronger documentation that his experience was indeed happening. It would certainly convince those who doubted his word and the evidence he held. Semjase's comment was direct and harsh and centered on those few people who prefer to turn their minds off rather than give it the minimal exercise of thought. She had warned him that some would accept the experience as an absolute, a few would question before they made a decision, and others would never believe, even if a ship were to land on their porch.

Other people were considered too negative and labeled as having "auric stench," a distasteful phrase that describes the negative energies that emanate from "Earth-humans," often without their knowledge or conscious thought. These frequencies create a state of altered equilibrium in the Pleiadian being and, for this reason, are monitored carefully. Billy laughed aloud as he recalled people whom he had come in contact with who, through their mere presence, had given him a horrid headache.

Pertaining to proof, it was not Meier's duty, nor theirs, nor anyone else's, to forcefully coerce or argue the existence of extraterrestrial life. The forms of evidence had been given not to convince but because there were men with open minds who needed some form of reality to trigger an inner recognition of fact.

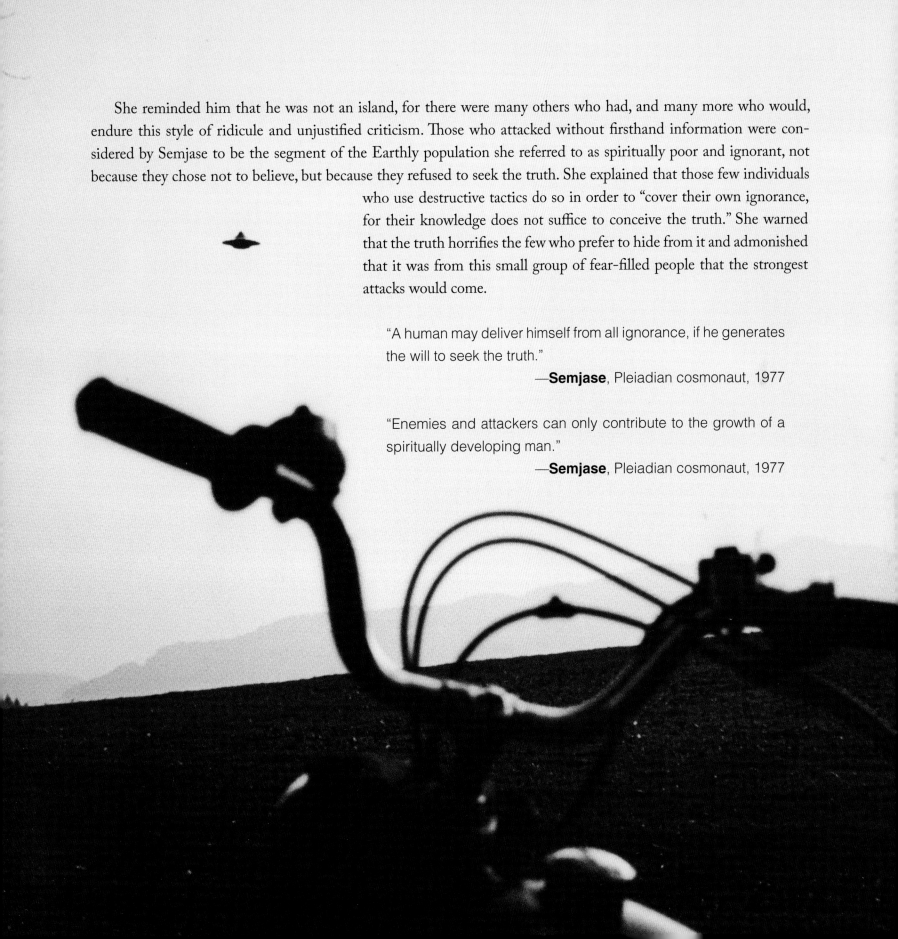

She reminded him that he was not an island, for there were many others who had, and many more who would, endure this style of ridicule and unjustified criticism. Those who attacked without firsthand information were considered by Semjase to be the segment of the Earthly population she referred to as spiritually poor and ignorant, not because they chose not to believe, but because they refused to seek the truth. She explained that those few individuals who use destructive tactics do so in order to "cover their own ignorance, for their knowledge does not suffice to conceive the truth." She warned that the truth horrifies the few who prefer to hide from it and admonished that it was from this small group of fear-filled people that the strongest attacks would come.

"A human may deliver himself from all ignorance, if he generates the will to seek the truth."

—**Semjase**, Pleiadian cosmonaut, 1977

"Enemies and attackers can only contribute to the growth of a spiritually developing man."

—**Semjase**, Pleiadian cosmonaut, 1977

On March 3, 1975, Meier was summoned into the third photographic session that defied the imagination of the Swiss farmer. The Pleiadians arrived this time with four beamships, two of the seven-meter variation and two of the remote-controlled type that were utilized extensively for certain monitoring assignments.

As the magnificent ships approached a beautiful Swiss valley, they slowly wheeled to pass directly overhead, allowing Meier the opportunity to film the flying formation. All of these crafts were new to Billy except the larger one on the right which was being taken out of service and being replaced by a newer variation of the same class seen at the lower left of the four-ship formation.

No landing took place on this occasion, but Meier was allowed to take an entire roll of slide transparencies as the beamships posed for his camera momentarily, before heading out to destinations unknown.

Many discussions often centered on the Pleiadian beamship and its means of propulsion, both of which the cosmonaut explained without detailed specifications. Unfortunately, Billy's lack of a formal education limited the questions he posed but undaunted, he continued to try and seek answers that might be comprehended by men of science. His persistence was continually rewarded with over-simplified answers, which were prefaced by the statement that there were many things that people of his planet had to grow into and learn from, and that their development would not progress if every speck of information was given to them.

In the text of what Semjase did choose to impart, it was disclosed that the Pleiadians utilize the disc-shaped craft because it offers many outstanding and unique capabilities for space flight, which includes the least resistance to air and friction. The beamship is surrounded by a "beam protection belt," or force field, which offers optimal safety and privacy as this unseen energy that envelopes the ship also offers a powerful and impenetrable screening device that prevents people and even radar from seeing the ships. The device may be turned off completely or partially, allowing only a segment of the craft to become visible.

In the winter of 1975, Semjase gave Meier the most thorough explanation of the propulsion system to date. Two independent systems are necessary: normal drive and hyper-drive. The first, a "light-emitting device," permits safe navigation in or out of a system of planetary bodies and an acceleration of speed where they may then make the hyper-jump: a multi-process method of travel in which the object moves many times faster than the speed of light.

The Pleiadian stated that the mass of an object increases in relationship to the speed that it travels, and here is where the first procedure of a hyperspace leap becomes a necessity. The ship is protected by the screens, which prevent the "mass-speed correlation." When the energy-field screens are withdrawn and the jump is made, the computers onboard simultaneously accelerate the "essential distortion unit" that then creates dematerialization. Space and time become paralyzed as one, and in the instant it requires to create a thought, the beamship rematerializes at its destination.

March 3, 1975, 10:00 hours
Location: Jacobsberg-Allenberg
The four ships, two seven-meter variations and two of the five-meter remote class, pass overhead. The series continues on pages 104–105.

"The Earth-humans' interest in space is just beginning to awaken, but it will take a great deal to maintain the knowledge and discover the many secrets that await these pioneers."

—**Ptaah**, Pleiadian cosmonaut, 1975

The journey from the Pleiades to Earth requires a trip of seven hours, which they feel is too lengthy in covering the almost five hundred light years. However, it was noted that Pleiadian scientists continue to develop new means of transportation systems which will decrease the seven hours currently needed to possibly minutes for future travel.

Semjase, when pressed for more detail by Meier concerning the workings of their propulsion system, replied that many scientists of Earth were working in the proper direction, with a few working on the light-emitting device for speeds up to the speed of light and others were developing a "tachyon" system that would establish a basis for hyper-space travel. The cosmonaut said that different names are used in her world, but the principles are the same and that was all that was important, with the exception of a stern warning of the dangers a civilization can open itself to in the early development of these techniques. The breakthrough of light speed without the use or knowledge of hyper-space, time dilations, and mass-speed correlations are but a few of the perils that could bring catastrophe to a ship and crew. All of these difficulties had been experienced by their ancestors, but without the disasters, they feel they would not have been able to collect knowledge and experience in space flight, which she compared to the mistakes and inaccurate calculations of the early missile programs in the 1950s.

"The Earth-human has reached the moon with missiles and the depths of the solar system with satellites but, he has yet to reach cosmic space."

—**Semjase**, Pleiadian cosmonaut, 1975

The energy screens mentioned earlier are similar to those utilized by the crew to prevent the neighboring towns-people from viewing the beamship as it maneuvers through the atmosphere. This light-reflection process of disappearing from sight has been described by witnesses as "blinking out." One moment the object was visible; the next it was not.

The contacts had become a commonplace event in the life of the farmer but as they continued, he began to experience a tremendous difficulty re-entering his own realm of existence. The extreme contrast of technology, beliefs, and ideals of the two worlds made the transition even more formidable. He knew that they had overcome the troublesome dilemmas that now faced his world. He knew that they had suffered through their learning stages until conscious arduous decisions were made by all to work together. Once this occurred, they were prepared to accept responsibility for themselves and their actions and other beings were there to assist. He was also aware that help cannot be given to those who will not help themselves first.

The Pleiadians had already chosen their path to advancement and had navigated the ups, downs, and curves, which were in their development. They had witnessed a great civilization destroyed and understood that there were no guarantees when they settled Erra, but as a unified group that wished to survive, they had managed to grow and mature into a harmonious society.

"The Earth-human, who has consciously allowed himself to reason and think, has walked forward in the steps of evolution. Today, he has stepped out of this level and has gained greater reasoning and understanding. Evolution demands that he makes use of these forces…but indeed, they are only utilized to their full extent through spiritual development."

—**Semjase**, Pleiadian cosmonaut, 1976

March 18, 1975, 09:07 hours
Location: Winkelriet

The Pleiadians told Meier that their civilization, advanced as it is, is not unique in structure and compared their lifestyle to that of the population on Earth.

They live in a single-family dwelling that is circular, self-sufficient, and located on an ample plot of land that is fertile and easily cultivated. Each family produces its own garden filled with the dietary staple of Erra, vegetables. All infertile land is utilized for the construction of large round buildings that house technical and sociological centers.

A baby entered the world of Erra in the identical manner children of Earth are born, with one major exception—chemicals to suppress pain are never introduced to the mother's body, as this could not only cause ill effects in the mother but the child as well. The predominant responsibility for the early development of the child rests with the mother, although both parents share in the rearing. Like an Earth child, the Erra child must grow and learn and, once they are old enough, they begin their education—a minimum of seventy years of day-to-day schooling. This is an obligation of the parents that is overseen by a "high council." Once the child has matured, they will choose a career that will fit their skills and natural talents and therefore will remain a pleasurable working situation. Their lessons are not strictly focused on only the technical aspects of their future but consist as well in teaching coexistence with nature and the Creational forces. They must learn early in life that they cannot permit either side to overpower the other but instead achieve the goal of balance between the material-spiritual world in which they live.

Research and evolution played a decisive role in advancing their life span, as their society had spent a great deal of time isolating, preventing, and curing diseases. In the case of an accident where an individual loses an internal organ or a limb, an artificial replacement is constructed. Recognizing the fact that no two physical bodies contain the identical chemical-mineral components, the Pleiadians prefer not to utilize donated organs for transplant purposes, thus preventing an imbalance in the physical body. Evolution has brought about "gene conditioning," a sophisticated exchange where the genes regulate the cells, and the cells, in turn, regulate the regeneration and disintegration of the life form.

Ecology and land management are shown full respect, and the laws encompassing them are rigidly adhered to by all. Mining and other such operations that can alter the delicate equilibrium of a planet are carried out on uninhabitable worlds that, although they cannot support life, may be rich in needed mineral deposits.

The most unique item in the Pleiadian society, as compared with that which Meier was accustomed to, was that no matter what the developed work skills of an individual may be, they receive no monetary consideration or reward for their endeavors. This was difficult for a man like Meier to comprehend, but money or its equivalent had not been used for centuries, as all Pleiadians are compensated by having their basic needs provided for. Families are self-sustaining, and as a whole, the society accepts responsibility for all that happens around them. The theory of "you are your brother's keeper" indeed seems to hold true and be the ruling force of this organized culture.

March 8, 1975, 17:40 hours
Location: Ober-Sadelegg

"The only thing limiting the progress of the Earth-human is the Earth-human himself."

—**Semjase**, Pleiadian cosmonaut, 1977

March 3, 1975, 17:00 hours
Location: Ober-Zelg

March 28, 1976, 16:50 hours
Location: Bachtelhornli
This series (pages 112–114) shows
one seven-meter craft and two five-
meter remotes as they move across
the horizon.

Time after time he followed the telepathic impulses during the ensuing months, returning home after each event with rolls and rolls of undeveloped film and reports of the phenomenally detailed conversations with the beings whose homeland was known as Erra. The unworldly contacts took place at all hours of the day and night, leaving substantial evidence in their wake, including literally hundreds of remarkably clear photographs, landing tracks or "footprints of the beamships," bushes that had been seared from coming in direct contact with the craft, physical samples of a metallic material and mineral specimens, and over a dozen eyewitnesses who substantiated his story, some having had the opportunity to film the ship before or after an encounter.

Billy Meier's experiences have become the longest series of documented contacts ever recorded. In the spring of 1978, he had had a total of 105 face-to-face meetings with the visitors, with the events continuing to produce a host of remarkable and unparalleled evidence.

After many of the meetings, the Pleiadian craft was observed by numerous witnesses who were astounded by the reality of the claimed events. The eye-opening experiences created needed support for the quiet Swiss farmer whose sanity was previously questioned at the mere mention of the encounters. But such was the nature of the events as first reported. As the meetings continued and the attention on them increased, the tranquil rural communities of Canton Zurich were forever disturbed by the historical proportions of the experiences that could no longer be ignored.

Meier's closest friends had urged him to bring his photographs and encounters to the attention of the

"A spiritually developing person is a noble artist of precious spirit, soft character, full of love, knowledge, wisdom, and logic. He is most sensible in the development of truth, beauty, and spiritual progress.

"His life is orderly, clarified, and above this, his perspectives are very extensive. His whole being is generous and beauty expresses herself in his unpretentious life of spiritual dignity. His inner calm holds a beauty, which no artist is able to capture on canvas and no poet is able to describe in words. His tranquility exercises a force of attraction, which even the most harmonious music cannot express. His self-assurance is unequaled, and his goals and aims hold no limitations.

"His wisdom is an always-present light, shining even into the darkest depths. It is not like the light of day, which can be overcome by the darkness of night.

"His presence is always the incense of eternity, which never fades away, while the fragrance of the most beautiful rose or orchid pines away and disappears into the time of endlessness."

—**Semjase**, Pleiadian cosmonaut, 1977

"One cannot clothe love into words, for love is the same as bliss, a state without a place. It is imperishable and cannot be shaped or manipulated into what it is not."

—**Semjase**, Pleiadian cosmonaut, 1976

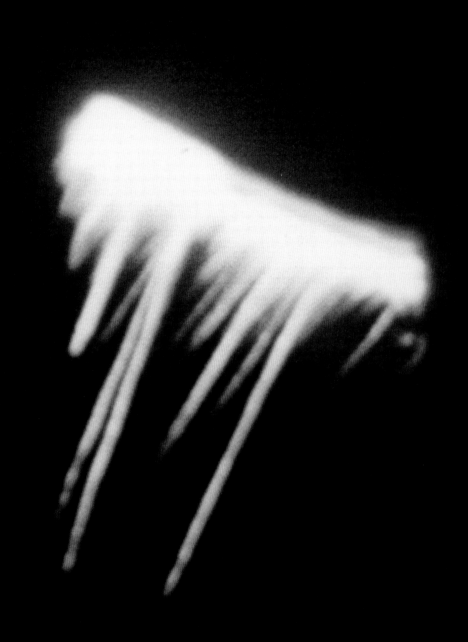

June 13,1976
This photograph is a night shot taken by Guido, one of many witnesses to the Meier events.

The Witnesses

Eduard "Billy" Meier and his wife, Kalliope, 1978

A number of the witnesses gather at the farmhouse to be interviewed by the investigators, 1978.

Meier leaving the farm on his moped, 1980

"One eye-witness is of more weight than ten hearsays."
—**Plautus**

From the early beginning of the Meier contacts to the present, there have been numerous individuals who have sought out the man to learn more about the events, and with some, the events became very real and profound and eventually they too became witnesses.

The following statements are taken from the exact words of the witnesses:

"In Hinwil, when I arrived, there were already a number of people gathered at the Meier household…After a short planning discussion we departed about 01:00 AM, following Billy on his moped to the scheduled landing place of the spacecraft. Arriving, we immediately set our cameras facing a northeast direction, toward the woods. At exactly 2:15 AM, the night performance started in the sky.

"As was determined prior, it began in the northeast direction, in front of a forested hill. A reddish disc-shaped light glowed brightly then went out. After a short pause, a silver disc a little bit higher was seen, but it was directly over the position of the first, and almost the same size and intensity. Soon after that, a third disc-shaped light appeared in a higher position. The ladies in our group said that this one had three colors, but I personally didn't see this because I was working with my camera to adjust its elevation.

Atlantis Meier showing an illustration of one of the objects he has seen, 1979.

Meier discussing aspects of the case with Lee Elders and Thom Welch, 1980.

Brit Elders talking with Kalliope and Elsi, a witness, 1979.

"Soon high over the horizon there came a silver disc that had a glittering rain of fire falling straight down and was spectacular in its display. Finally, after this demonstration we could see the spacecraft flying away slowly as it withdrew to a small red point of light in the sky. Then it ascended rapidly and disappeared. The whole expedition did not take more than ten minutes. This was, according to Meier and others present, the fifty-fifth contact since January 28, 1975."

—**Guido**, school superintendent, Austrian

"I watched it go to the right, then left; then the light turned off. It wasn't the moon; the moon was bright but different. I painted a picture of it in school."

—**Atlantis Meier**, student, Swiss, 1978

"That morning when I went to pick up Billy, I drove up the hill…I saw Quetzel's new ship…very close."

—**Eva**, secretary, Swiss, 1980

"It was white and big…very big and went up and down. One time it went to the left; the rest of the time it went up and down. I called to Jakobus, and we watched it for ten minutes."

—**Gilgamesha Meier**, student, Swiss, 1979

"My main interest is in the notes and the information they give…How many times have I seen a craft? Too many times to remember."

–**Maria**, office manager, Swiss, 1980

"In June of 1976, seven people were waiting with me for Billy to come back from a contact. He came and said to us, 'Go with me to another point.' We went and waited. It was daylight, and one of the boys told us to look up into the sky. It was our first sighting in the day. The ship was very big but got smaller as it rose, and I clearly saw the detail around the top of the ship. I saw little ports, and the whole UFO seemed to be light. The children, three other women, and one man saw it too. There are many lights going across the sky at night and I cannot be sure what they are, but this I am sure was the ship of Semjase. I didn't believe it before because I had never talked about UFOs or seen one. But after this day... I believe.

"Now the UFOs are secondary, the information from the Pleiadians come first. We have to learn to live together...man and woman, different countries, different races, and different worlds."

—**Kalliope Meier**, housewife, Swiss, 1979

"The continuous downpour soaked us through and through. Suddenly, we heard the hooting of an owl and seconds later, there started a peculiar sound, like leaves rustling in the wind. But there were only pines around, then this rustle turned into an increasing roar. A kind of whining. Then, suddenly, we saw Mr. Meier in the midst of us. He was smiling happily and in absolutely dry clothes. I saw by the headlights of the car, his leather coat getting wet slowly."

—**Engelbert**, printer, Swiss, 1980

Meier answers questions from John Wesley Roberts, 1980.

"I drove Billy to the contact site where I fell asleep shortly after he walked toward the woods. I was awakened by the shrill sound of Semjase's beamship and jumped out of the car to look around. It was raining very hard, but there, at the back of the auto, was Billy. Completely dry...the first raindrops dotting his coat."

—**Bernadette**, computer technician, Swiss, 1979

Brit interviewing witnesses, 1980.

"It happened February 7, 1977. I was waiting for Edi [Billy] during a contact...suddenly I startled! Quite suddenly and like magic, there appeared on the right side of my car, a human figure...materializing from the feet up! I was absolutely shaken, I tell you! It was Edi standing in front of me!"

—**Jakobus**, farmer, Swiss, 1980

"A glowing object of great size came in and moved slowly through the valley at the bottom of the hill last night about one o'clock. It wasn't an airplane; I have never seen a circular airplane."

—**Visitor from Holland**, taken from an interview the following morning with Lee Elders, 1979

Welch, Col. Stevens, and Elders with the contactee and his wife, 1980.

March 29, 1976, 19:50 hours
Location: Hasenbol-Langenberg
This still was taken from a frame of the 8mm movie footage. Note: the "hot spots" seen on the bottom of the craft. At first it was thought that these were reflections from sunlight but, after computer analysis, it was determined that they were an integral part of the ship.

The amazing properties revealed in the old 8mm movie film taken by Meier in 1975–76 became the turning point in the investigation for many of those involved. It would signal in a new era of knowledge to be learned and offer a new challenge for those with that need to know. The film contained subliminal clues, perhaps planted by this higher form of intelligence.

The Investigation Continues

"Progress is not created by contented people."

—**Frank Tyger**

For the American investigators it had literally been mind-boggling since they had first arrived on the scene to begin their time-consuming and exhaustive search into probing for the truth behind the Meier experiences. They had discovered early that the reality or nonreality of the Meier events could not be determined by intellectual debate or opinion for whatever was in fact happening was leaving its traces behind. It was these traces, the physical evidence that required analysis with the best tools available. So, time and time again they found themselves returning to the wide valley of Berg-Rumlikon, the rolling meadows of Ober-Sadelegg, and the wind-swept mountain at Hasenbol—these were the contact sites, those mystical places with the strange-sounding names.

The truly remarkable nature of this case came from the numerous forms of physical evidence awaiting examination. To objective but cautious minds it was like pieces of an elaborate jigsaw puzzle strewn about the Swiss landscape that

Summer 1982
Location: Hinterschmidruti
Eduard "Billy" Meier and Lee Elders discuss the trials and tribulations of a contactee, 1980.

Summer 1982
Location: Mountain ridge at Hasenbol
Elders, Col. Stevens, Meier, and Welch return to one of the most spectacular contact sites. It was here that the contactee filmed the series sequence seen on pages 116–120.

perhaps had been placed there with purpose and design, only awaiting the right person with the correct investigative procedures to unlock the keys to their mysterious meaning.

The Americans had exhausted most avenues of normal investigation procedures concerning the contact sites and the possible human manipulation of the photo-events by the use of models. Each site had its own "signature," or comparative reference points, such as trees, mountains or other known objects that would allow computer science the opportunity to compare the size and distance of the "knowns" against the "unknown" (the beamship). This combined information was fed to numerous optical science laboratories and engineers who were busy examining the farmer's photo-proofs with their high-tech computers and sophisticated software programs designed purposely for finding "the string" or the "paste-up." But time and time again the end results were always the same: a large object some distance from the camera.

It was now time to discard old investigative techniques and search behind the scenes at the contact zones for clues that would continue to reinforce Meier's claims. At the Frecht Natural Preserve, near Betzholz-Hinwil, the first major scientific clue surfaced. It was here on January 28, 1975, that the first contact had taken place, but even more importantly, the Pleiadian spacecraft had landed and was on the ground for more than one hour.

This area was quickly targeted for detailed examination by utilizing European state-of-the-art gamma ray detection equipment that had been provided by a major Swiss high-tech company. The results of the findings were shocking. RAD readings were detected within the contact zone perimeter one to five times above the norm. Even more startling, the gamma waves being detected came in short but powerful bursts, indicating that something awesome and perhaps undefinable had changed the molecular structure of the immediate area for years to come.

Spring 1980
Meier and Jun-Ichi Yaoi during filming of the Nippon Television Special that was aired to over thirty million Japanese in July and August of 1980.

In July of 1979, Intercep, the security firm responsible for protecting the physical evidence of the case, was contacted by the Nippon Television Network of Tokyo, Japan. The Japanese, aware of the Meier experiences, had offered to assist in the investigation, providing they were allowed to film a television special of their in-depth findings. Permission was granted, and soon one of that country's foremost investigator/reporters, Mr. Jun-Ichi Yaoi, entered the case, bringing with him over twenty years of accumulated knowledge and expertise concerning UFOs. Yaoi, who would spend over two weeks with the farmer, summed him up as follows: "a honest man living in a simple way."

When Jun-Ichi and his six-man film crew first arrived at the old farmhouse in Schmidruti, they appeared curious but unmoved, until the 8mm movie footage of the beamship was projected on the wall of the Meier living room. It was in this setting that the first of many surprises would come for them. The first sequence was daylight footage that showed a beamship hovering over a large pine tree beside a farmhouse, and as the sleek spacecraft began slowly to circle around and over the giant pine, constantly accelerating in speed, a very unusual movement was detected. As the ship made its third pass over the weather pine, the top branches of the tree were seen to sway violently from the backwash of the flying object. The East-West investigative team was stunned but also highly elated for this was the kind of hard evidence that they had hoped for.

The next revelation was even more exciting and came in the sequence showing a disc-shaped Pleiadian beamship hovering over the Berg-Rumlikon valley in the summer of 1975 (see movie camera scene in volume I on pages 62–63). This remarkably clear film shows the spacecraft gently floating on the air current; then without warning it suddenly "blinks out" of the frame, disappearing from view for a period of twenty-eight seconds. At first, it was thought that the film had been cut, but under close examination in NTV's laboratory in Japan, this was found to be untrue. Further analysis uncovered something highly unusual, for at the exact moment the ship vanished an unusual "light shift" occurred, and the entire scene or visible spectrum became "shaded." It was almost as if an invisible "umbrella" had screened out direct light. The scene remained "filtered" until the beamship reappeared; then amazingly the lighting returned to normal. When Meier was asked about this extraordinary phenomenon, he simply replied, "The Pleiadians use an electromagnetic force field to bend light away from their ships and this protection belt prevents unwarranted observation."

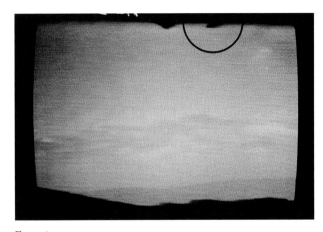

Frame 1.
Prior to "jump."
Beamship is seen in upper right corner.

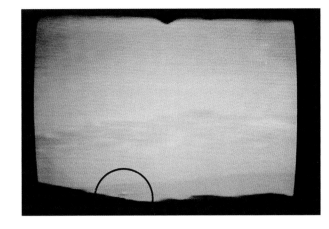

Frame 2.
"Jump."
Beamship is now seen in lower corner to the left of center, in the beginning stages of materialization.

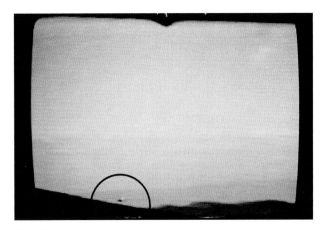

Frame 3.
After "jump."
Beamship is now clearly defined and fully materialized.

The most exciting discovery came after the movie footage was transferred to videotape and taken back to the Nippon Television facilities in Tokyo. Utilizing extreme slow-motion techniques combined with freeze-frame analysis, the beamship is seen materializing in stages (frames 2 and 3) after the jump or dematerializing.

Considering the fact that the Pleiadians were indeed light years ahead of Earth-human technology contributed to their remarkable capabilities of being able to "bend light" away from the beamships. Their stealth program offered them a high degree of protection from the prying eyes of radar and outsiders. Also, it seemed quite natural that light and electromagnetic disturbances were associated with the operation of the sleek beamships within the Earth's atmosphere. Isolated events of the past that had been noted in Meier's diary indicated that mechanical equipment such as tractors and mopeds failed to function properly in the near vicinity of a close encounter. It was also common knowledge to those around Meier that clocks, compasses, and watches with calendar mainsprings ran forward and backward at odd times. Normally this was found to be true during contact periods, but sometimes a simple courtesy call or flyby would set off the unusual behavior. While the electromagnetic problems and their consistent patterns could easily be documented by numerous witnesses and rationalized by progressive and open minds, one puzzling aspect still remained a mystery. What was the nature of the powerful electromagnetic field, and was it related to propulsion? How did the Pleiadians accomplish such staggering distances of space travel?

These questions led to conversations with two prominent and dedicated science investigators: Mr. H. David Froning, who represented a major aerospace company's propulsion research division, and Mr. Alan Holt, an independent researcher and consultant to America's space program. Both men had published technical papers on their work in recent years that resulted in a more thorough understanding of the questions now being posed.

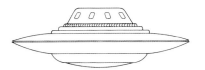

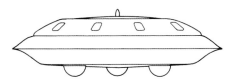

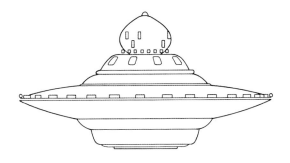

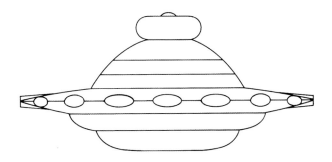

The field resonance propulsion system, which Holt referred to as an extension of the Einstein unified field theory, was said to be most effective in a spacecraft design that was circular and disc-shaped. The design was developed around factors required by the propulsion system and the various expectations of interstellar travel. Surprisingly, it was coincidentally similar to the shapes seen in thousands of recorded UFO sightings from around the world. In operation, the field resonance vehicle would start generating an energy pattern as it lifts off the ground. This energy pattern would initially cause an ionization or glow around the craft that would begin as red in color, then later the energy field would increase in energy and frequency, turning blue, violet, and a brilliant white just before dematerialization from that point in space and time to reappear at another point in space and time.

The statements from Alan Holt were of great interest because they were highly consistent with not only the design of the Pleiadian beamships but also shed light on the witnesses' accounts of what they had been seeing and filming over the

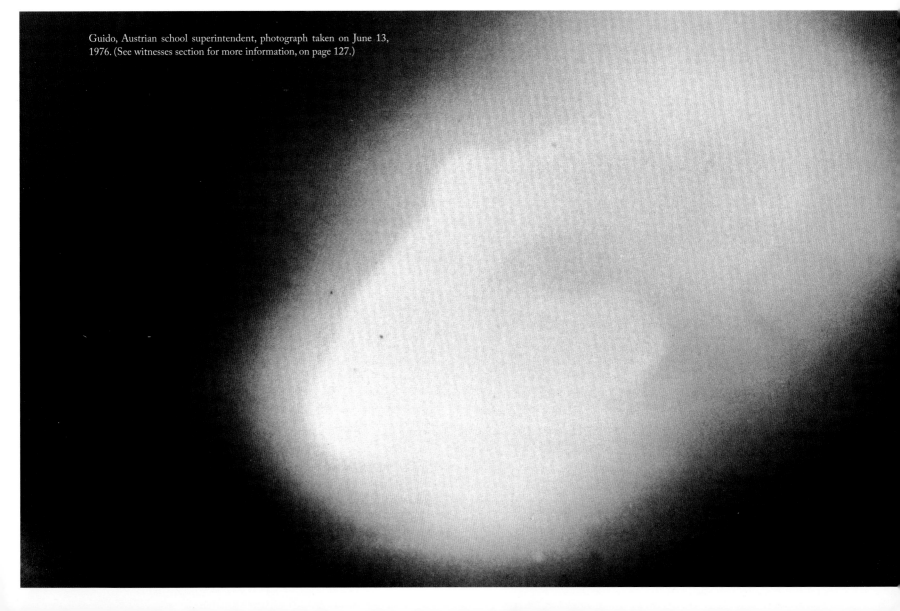

Guido, Austrian school superintendent, photograph taken on June 13, 1976. (See witnesses section for more information, on page 127.)

February 7, 1979
Location: Zurich International Airport at Kloten
Photographer unknown. Note: Compare the corona of light
and the shape of craft with the photo on the previous page.

rural countryside of Switzerland for the past few years. As well, David Froning's extrapolation of the time required using these systems of travel between the Earth and the Pleiades star cluster was estimated at approximately eight hours—an amazing coincidence, for seven years prior to Froning statement, and unknown to Froning, Meier had recorded in his notes that the Pleiadians make their journey to Earth in seven hours, a remarkable one-hour difference!

Froning and Holt described a revolutionary form of instantaneous interstellar travel involving other dimensions, where particles can travel unrestricted many times the speed of light. The system produces the visual characteristics of materialization and dematerialization within "pieces of a second," as Meier referred to it. It is also accompanied by light distortions and shifts, including glowing and ionization of brilliant colors that seem to engulf the spacecraft. As one prominent scientist put it, "If indeed these spacecrafts were capable of interdimensional travel, then it would stand to reason, that when they entered our three-dimensional world, surprising phenomena would occur."

This photograph of a glowing disc-shaped object engulfed in an intense ball of light was taken over Zurich International Airport at Kloten in February of 1979, by an unidentified woman seeing her daughter off on a flight in a Boeing 747 wide-bodied transport. She snapped the picture with a Polaroid camera and when she saw the developed print, went immediately to a newsstand in the air terminal, bought an envelope, and mailed the print to *Blick*, a local newspaper. There is no evidence that this person ever heard of Billy Meier. Professional photographers who have examined the print are unable to explain the phenomenon by any known process. This photograph closely resembles the beautiful night shot taken by the Austrian school superintendent near Chalberweid in June 1976.

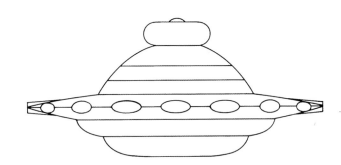

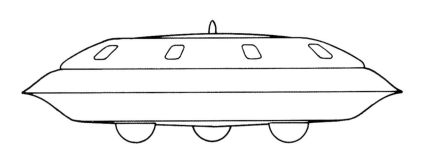

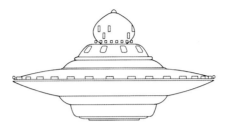

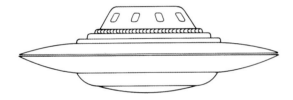

Footprints

"If the Earth could talk, what a tale it could tell."

—**Anonymous**

The footprints (landing tracks) of the sleek disc-shaped Pleiadian beamship were observed and recorded on film during the highly active contact years of 1975–76, when the alien cosmonauts preferred to touchdown for their meetings.

The Pleiadian seven-meter ships—variations 1 through 4—had landed on tripod legs that were extended from the lower surface of the craft. These legs have circular-shaped pads that left a round swirled-down pattern in the grass of two meters in diameter. The pilotless, remote-controlled vehicles, utilized for mechanical and electronic monitoring purposes, are three to five meters in size but landed on three hemispherical structures that were spaced 120 degrees apart on their circular undersides. When settled, they too rest on disc-shaped shoes that leave the grass and vegetation swirled down in a counterclockwise direction; however, it was observed that all of the interplanetary beamships were very seldom maneuvered into a full landing position, preferring instead to hover a few centimeters above the surface. Yet, when full touchdown was necessary, the shoe pads showed the same "anti-oscillation" (counterclockwise rotation print) as the smaller remote-controlled vehicles. The anti-oscillation print baffled the observers, including Meier, until on the sixtieth contact when the question was answered by the cosmonaut Semjase.

It was explained that the round surface areas of the support legs also vibrate as a part of the entire spaceship, in a spiral shaped anti-gravity oscillation. Each ship has four such vortex centers, three at the landing pads and the fourth being the bottom center of the spaceship itself. This would explain the many single footprints observed in the snow during winter contacts.

Another question that nudged the senses was why grass and bushes affected by the vortex centers continued to thrive and grow in a counterclockwise motion long after a contact had occurred. It was explained that the "anti-gravity oscillation" of the beamship is more powerful than the normal gravitational field of planet Earth; thus the new force field overcomes the gravitational force field of our planet and creates in the plant life a gravitational shift which the plant assumes is correct. This counter-gravity force then lingers for a period of time until it becomes weakened through age and then Earth's gravity once again takes command.

October 1980
Location: Hinterschmidruti
Meier observes the tracks at the site where a large seven-meter beamship landed the night before. Gamma testing at this site revealed a RAD count well above normal almost two years after this photo was taken.

Pertaining to the footprints, one mystery still remains—hundreds of different types of insects seem to be drawn to the inner circle of the vortex center and seem to thrive within the circle for days. One scientist concluded that perhaps there is a residue of ultraviolet light attracting these creatures, and if so, then it is quite possible that the Pleiadian beam-ships utilize this light source as a product or byproduct of their energy needs.

"I am very, very sure, there is no way for Billy to make tracks like this. I have been many times a witness of these landing tracks, and I have very clear photos in all details from many different places so I can say this to you by all safety, 100 percent. There is a place in Switzerland that a spaceship landed in 1976…and after four years today, you can see the grass in this place growing differently from other grass…"

—**Herbert**, West Germany, 1980

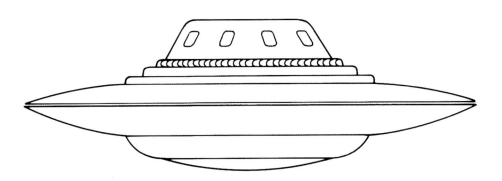

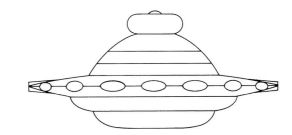

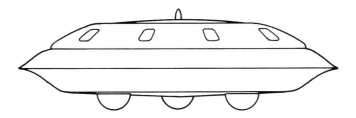

Science

Science is defined as "systematized knowledge derived from observation," a method of turning previous mysteries into an evolving yet understandable collection of knowns. The scientific path represented an area of potential discovery and exciting exploration that could be traversed by utilizing the tools of twentieth-century technology which would allow in-depth study of the photographs, spacecraft sounds, and the metal samples—with skill, luck, and the true nature of the hard evidence left in the wake of the Meier experience, all would be solved. However, combining science with the age-old mystery referred to as the UFO phenomenon would be the first major obstacle to be overcome.

In three decades of UFO monitoring and recordkeeping, a number of seemingly unbelievable facts had continued to surface, which reinforced the problems related to private sector investigation into UFO associated events. First, the subject matter remained imbedded in a very general and misleading catch-all category, sharing equal billing with monsters, myths, mysteries, and other unknown and unexplainable phenomenon. Unlike other areas of the human experience, little more was generally known by the public today about these things than when they first came to the public's attention in 1947. Also contributing to the knowledge gap was the fury of differing opinions and the sheer force of continued mislabeling, premature rejection of legitimate cases, and hasty generalization that created an unbelievable nightmare of questionable credibility that quite frankly had proved to be too intimidating and had frightened away many a prominent and dedicated scientist. UFO research from a scientific level was nonexistent, suffering from a lack of systematized knowledge and void of scientific observation which contributed heavily to its stigma-ridden image.

The circumstances surrounding the Meier case were as intimidating as those of its brothers from the past. Perhaps even more so! The case entered the stigma-ridden world of ufology bursting with hard evidence that could be tested by modern-day science, but to the dismay of those with the need to know, it found itself totally alone, ignored by the media, major industry, government, and science. To make matters worse, it was even shunned by the community that was dedicated to its research. In the investigative language of the UFO community, the Meier events had been labeled a "repeater case" because of the continuing reoccurrence of the contacts themselves. Those who dominated opinion in the UFO field stressed the fact that "repeater cases" were improbable and illogical and most likely were created by individuals with self-serving interests. This was the intellectual environment in which the Meier case first appeared.

The journey down the scientific path in search of science integrity would in the beginning be lonely and difficult. It would eventually become a strong test of endurance for all those concerned with many pitfalls of frustration that would last for years to come. Patience became the byword, but later the interest level in those mysterious artifacts from another place and another time would begin to swell, and eventually new doors would be opened allowing access to the necessary equipment and expertise to see the job through.

The mixture of evidence and attitude ultimately attracted the perfect chemistry of science and technology. To those who defied the stigma and the possible damage to their own reputations, the opportunity was so rare that it could no longer be ignored…Indeed the search for science integrity was not conducted by contented people.

Metal Analysis

By mid-summer of 1979, the Pleiadian metal samples had already undergone initial elemental analysis by two major metallurgical laboratories in Switzerland and Arizona. From Europe came a standard report that listed lead and silver in major parts and a host of trace materials. Nothing unusual was discovered by the Swiss, and their report was somewhat mundane in nature. In Arizona a more detailed analysis was in progress, and the first of many surprises were beginning to surface. The sand-like granules were the first to be examined and were found to be non-metallic and generally uniform in size and sub-angular shape. Meier had said earlier that these pieces had once been a whole. This posed an interesting question. Had the rest of this mass oxidized away for some strange reason?

Such knowledge is remarkably widespread across the South American continent. Even the Abipones tribe of the Brazilian Amazon circle their protective jungle campfires and discuss the Pleiades with pride; after all, according to the "old ones," they are the source of their ancestors!

Pre-Inca religions and cultures reveal that much of the South American civilizations was based on the belief that their forefathers came from the stars and that these extraterrestrials taught the Incas how to use fire, as well as how to plant and harvest crops. In return for the greater knowledge that was imparted to them from their friends from the stars, the Incas built temples and constructed ceremonies to worship their mentors.

Fourth-state metal specimen, designated F-l by chemist Marcel Vogel. This mysterious specimen created an uproar within the scientific community because of its unusual bonding techniques. It showed a combination of both crystalline deposits and metal without evidence of crossbreeding, which was unheard of with the technology of the day. This piece mysteriously vanished while in the possession of Marcel Vogel.

"Matter is the embodiment of an idea."

—**Semjase**, Pleiadian cosmonaut, 1977

During another procedure when the third specimen was being mounted in a lucite crystal, the metallurgist noted an unexpected outflow of a gas-like-substance from the solid metal that fractured the crystal mounts. The scientist was shocked! He commented that he had never seen anything like it before, that it was highly unusual, and that it seemed to indicate that something was being "given up" by the metal at the low heat of the mounting process. This fragment, when studied more closely, could be polished to a very bright finish, but within a few minutes, it would oxidize back to its original unpolished dark color. This effect was observed in 16 percent humidity, which is extremely dry conditions for oxidization to occur. The other specimens did not oxidize, and once polished, they retained their brilliance.

Meier had received the metal samples during a contact in the late summer 1977, during his forty-sixth meeting with the cosmonaut Semjase. It was explained at the time that each specimen represented a different, yet consecutive, stage of development in the process of making Pleiadian metal for use in spacecraft production. The alloy utilized had a very different bonding technique, which required seven different and difficult development stages and that by our twentieth-century understanding would be impossible to duplicate. The cosmonaut had also stated, "At present, Earth technology could not build their rocket-like spacecraft using this alloy, but in order to understand its true value and exact need, Earth societies would first have to be capable of space flight similar to ours…and this information can but be only a suggestion to the Earth scientists for the still distant future."

From a metallurgical viewpoint, the analysis had reached its limit because the specimens could not be immediately identified as being usable in any known twentieth-century technical application, nor were they a byproduct of any known process.

The next challenge was to find an expert in optical and electron microscope study techniques (microscopy) who was familiar with various levels of scientific knowledge in crystal and metal technology. The search had its frustrations. But eventually a man of eminent qualifications was found, Marcel Vogel, a senior scientist with IBM. In Northern California, in the fall of 1979, after months of work on the specimens, Vogel agreed to summarize his findings for the American/Japanese investigative team by releasing his laboratory videotaped reports. The following are a few of his profound and documented statements.

"We are now at 600 diameters of magnification and now a whole new world appears in the specimen under polarized light, cross field. There are structures within structures that one sees, very, very unusual…at lower magnification and without oil, one just sees a metallic surface. Now one sees a structure, which is composed of various types of interlacing areas…here they are, being brought out, these are structures within structures. This is very exciting, very interesting, and bears looking into! We are at crossed-field…we are using the 250 Watt Zenon and Sisium iodide source…we go to a higher magnification yet…and higher yet…we are now at over 2500 (diameters) and one can see these birefringent (reflective crystalline) structures…very exciting! This is very unusual for a metal to have these birefringent areas. A metal normally will not exhibit this…

"When you first take a section and grind it off, it looks like a metal, it has a lustery appearance of the metal, now when you take that and you go under the polarized light and you study it, you find that yes, it is metal, but at the same time it is crystal. There are structures in there which are crystal, which are birefringent, which are non-metal…(the purity itself of each element) that is uncanny when you look at the juxtaposition of these metals to one another, when one layer against another is very pure but they did not interpenetrate into one another. They are not evaporated, they are like taffy that has been pulled, flowed…so you have a combination of metals and non-metals together and very tightly blended into one another. (This is unheard of)…I don't know of anybody even contemplating doing something like that.

"The major element which is shown here was the rare earth metal thulium, it was totally unexpected…that was only purified during World War II, and only in minute quantities…these are byproducts of the need that we have for certain rare earths in atomic energy work.

"…Combined with thulium was also [bromine]. There is a minute trace of silver and argon but no other secondary band…

"The metal thulium is rather rare to come by and would require pretty advanced technology for any person who were to try to conceive of it, to build a composite…if anybody wanted to make any sort of fake.

"Right now, I could not explain the type of material that I have and its discreteness by any known combination of materials…I could not put it together myself as a scientist. To get a combination of thulium, silver, and silicon in discrete areas…yes, if I were to melt it together, I would see the evidence of all of them, but their discreteness is what intrigues me. You understand what I am saying? Because, you see, if I would take these combinations of materials and put them into a furnace, melt it, and pour it out and pull a little ingot, I would see all of these elements present there in any one area, but I don't (in these). I see these discrete bits of material. Now it can only happen by some form of a cold fusion process where you have the elements present, and you fuse them together so they still maintain their (pure) identity but they interpenetrate into one another.

"Now we, with any technology that I know of, could not achieve this on this Earth planet. It is very exciting when you can get specimens like these and have the opportunity of looking at and examining them…it does not look like anything that we've made here."

This was to be the last statement made on the remarkable metal sample that had taken the scientific community by storm. The specimen vanished without a trace from its container while being hand-carried by Vogel to a new testing laboratory. To this day, the metal's whereabouts remains an unsolved mystery.

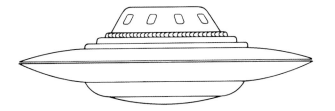

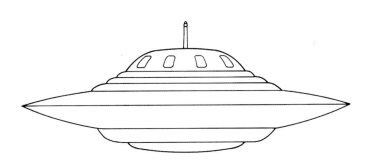

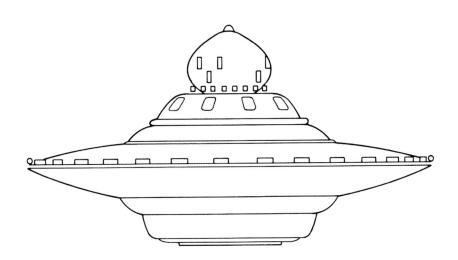

Sound Analysis

On April 24, 1976, Meier made his way to a relatively secluded area in anticipation of a prearranged contact scheduled for late afternoon. On this occasion he had been promised something very special, and he carried with him both a camera and a cassette tape recorder. What happened next was one of those rare occasions in UFO history when the pursuit of a beamship by a Swiss military Mirage jet fighter was both recorded on 35 mm film and audio recording tape at the same time (see pages 38–39).

The eerie sound of the UFO and of the other fixed-wing aircraft that was vectored in on the spacecraft were exciting and unprecedented, and offered excellent documentation with the usual noises of a dog barking, a crow cawing, and police sirens heard in the distance on the tape. However, it was determined that a more consistent sound, primarily the tone of the spacecraft was necessary without outside interference of mixed sounds if a thorough analysis was to be made. But "pure" sounds of the beamship were nonexistent and it would take almost four years before new sounds were obtained.

Then in the spring of 1980, the Pleiadians acknowledged the need and directed Billy, his family, and selected friends to the rolling meadow of Ober-Sadelegg where an amazing demonstration took place. With his wife, Kalliope, maintaining one tape recorder and Billy the other, they simultaneously recorded thirty minutes of beamship audio approximately three hundred yards apart. Surprisingly, both recordings matched in frequency and tone despite the distance between the two recorders. Yet, witnesses reported that no spacecraft was observed during the event and that the mystical yet awesome sound was all encompassing and even heard by farmers working in the adjacent fields. It was unlike anything on this planet, as scientist discovered.

> "I don't see any application for it, with the exception of generating a magnetic wave of some sort…or maybe in this case, propulsion."
>
> —**Rob Shellman**, sound engineer, 1982

Analyzing and attempting to identify the various components of the spacecraft sound would prove to be a formidable task. This sound was comprised of many tones, all changing extremely fast. The purest tone existed at approximately one thousand cycles per second accompanied by harmonics of that tone aligning with others to provide a uniform signal. But the excitement and interest came in the unusual anomaly of the rapid change in tones. As Mr. Steve Ambrose, a sound engineer and consultant, explained after staring at the visual display of the time domain and spectrum analyzers, "There are a hundred different changes every two or three seconds on here…There certainly aren't any synthesizers that have oscillators that are that many and that randomly tuned to that many random things, all changing simultaneously. That's not something inherent in any of the synthesizers that are used for professional recording or creating sound. This is something that has a tremendous amount of oscillation at different frequencies."

Curious patterns continued to appear as the audio engineers noted a whole range of frequencies all the way to the top of the audio range, with pure tones and their harmonics standing out from time to time. Of a peculiar nature was one correlation found during analysis, the significance of which is still unknown. One steady pattern continued to haunt the engineers, for it appeared throughout all the random signals, as it seemed to be a level change around five cycles per second. This was a frequency modulation that happened to be in the exact area of the natural magnetic resonance of the Earth, also referred to as the Schuman resonance. Was it possible that the UFO did ride the magnetic waves of our planet as Meier had reported in his notes way back in 1975?

Spring 1982
This photograph was taken from a video tape and shows the tones of the spacecraft sounds converging.

"It is not as though before you had ten different frequencies at random and then all of a sudden nine dropped out and you only had one left…What is happening is the ten different frequencies are converging on one central frequency which…I find very interesting…"

—**Nils Rognerud**, BSEE, April 1982

"The modulation beat that we hear on the tape, occurs at different frequency peaks…Each one of these peaks is a discrete frequency. The curious thing about this change is the number of changes…four, five, six, seven. All the way to a number that becomes difficult to discern. At a certain point you will generate a certain amount of magnetism, then you can select stronger fields of magnetism."

—**Rob Shellman**, sound engineer, 1982

"The sound pattern is very dynamic and changing, and the only thing that seemed to have a repeatable pattern was an amplitude-modulation (a signal in which the volume is varied at a low periodical rate). For the three UFO recordings, this frequency worked out to be 4.9 cycles per second, 4.6 cycles per second, and 5.0 cycles per second. It is worthwhile revealing that Nikola Tesla discovered a natural electro-magnetic resonance of Earth at 6.6 cycles per second. A second gentleman named Schuman also discovered a second resonance at 7.8 cycles per second. Now, these are all natural resonances, and it seems kind of interesting to note the UFO sounds having vibrations in a similar if not identical pitch…an associate of mine…has done some similar research. He researched a UFO-abduction case (in Texas) where the people involved were sitting in a car and a cassette-tape player happened to be playing music while the alien spacecraft was approaching. The tape was analyzed, and he found low frequency vibrations of 7.14 cycles, 4.72 cycles, and 3.52 cycles per second."

—A sound engineer's confidential report to Col. Stevens, December 12, 1981

Asked by the investigators if it would be possible to recreate this sound, in view of his detailed analysis, the professional sound analyst and engineer concluded: "To be honest with you, I personally don't think so. The signals are changing at such a fast rate…Possibly you could create a steady state, a random signal, with synthesizers, electronic instruments, but to add on the change on top of it is, I think, very difficult. There are no synthesizers on the market that have oscillators that change that randomly, even if you got nine or ten of them going, they wouldn't change from those peaks that quickly…Besides, if you were going to create a noise for a spaceship, you would be hard put to come up with something as original as this."

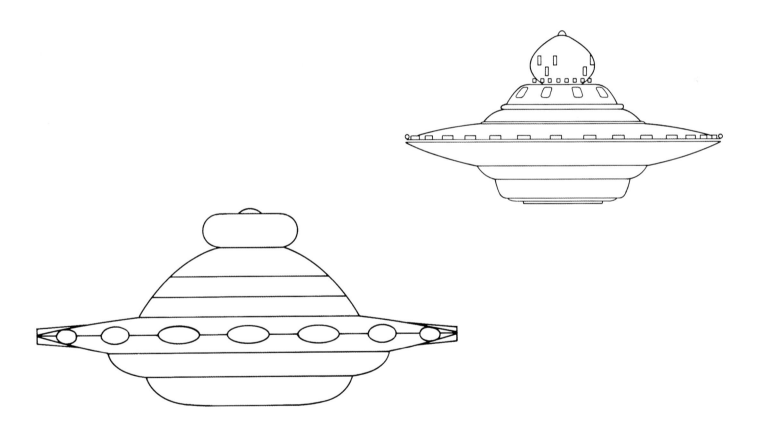

Photo Analysis

Separate from the Meier investigation activities, Intercep initiated a confidential probe into the existing state-of-the-art scientific equipment and research procedures that were applicable in testing UFO photographs. It eventually would lead to bringing in a special dedicated team of science investigators that were willing to accept the difficult challenge of pioneering this brave new world. The project was led by Jim Dilettoso, whose specialty was locating and implementing special computer hardware, software, laser components, and other highly specialized systems necessary to get the job done. The objective was twofold: to find the deception methods if they existed, and if not, to learn as much from the photo evidence as possible. This would require the science investigators to stay abreast of any new developments made in equipment and procedures concerning optical science, while at the same time gaining access to these state-of-the-art electronics.

This sounded easy, but finding the latest procedural knowledge and then gaining available time on all of this new equipment for the purpose of analyzing UFO photographs would become a formidable task. It would become an extensive and painstaking search, in some unique cases requiring years to locate necessary elements in this sophisticated category. This area of scientific application was very new, rising through its infantile stages and changing every two or three months in parallel with the advancing technical capabilities of graphics, computer, laser, and optical hardware.

The science investigators learned early that it was not enough to analyze photographs at a single level of technology, nor was it accurate to use general procedures which was then the practice of amateur activities in this field because the information being developed was in reality too general, requiring personal subjective opinions—this became too tempting in the politically charged atmosphere of ufology. Thus the decision was made to bypass the UFO community and instead concentrate on the new frontier of "high" science, where knowledge awaited the pioneers.

In order to initially determine the validity of the Meier photo-proofs, a photograph printed from the original transparency was submitted to a physicist working for a sub-contracting firm for the United States Navy and other government-contracted aerospace companies. The photograph was submitted for technical analysis utilizing the latest state-of-the-art photogrammetric analysis procedures. The scientist first examined the image field visually and micro-scopically to qualitatively evaluate the sharpness of the objects image and the scene. He found no discernible difference in image sharpness. Then color separation and black and white negatives were made at magnifications of one and ten, with the resulting negatives being processed by a scanning microdensitometer that yielded density contour plots. Next,

April 14, 1976, 16:11 hours
Location: Schmarbuel
This is the computer's point of view of the "jet-fighter scene," as seen on page 59. The image of the spacecraft has been enlarged to focus on the unusual field of red particles seen emitting from the ship. Scientists are still seeking an answer to this unexplained energy field.

Thermogram-color density separations and high-frequencies properties of light/time of day are correct: light values on the ground are reflected in craft bottom.

the print, color separation negatives, and black-and-white negatives were carefully examined for evidence of double exposure, photo paste-up, model at short range suspended on a string, etc. Through the state-of-the-art analysis procedures used in March of 1978, no evidence of hoaxing could be found. The physicist's report concluded that "nothing was found in the examination of the print which could cause me to believe that the object in the photo is anything other than a large object photographed a distance from the camera."

Further steps of analysis continued to be the goal of the dedicated science investigators as the technology and research capabilities made itself available. Another major breakthrough came as two of the internegatives made directly from the original transparencies were delivered to an Arizona laser optics laboratory for emulsion study and experimentation (see pages 58–59). Of particular interest was analysis of the crystalline emulsion structure in the key portions of these photographs where the edges of the disc-shaped craft met with the background, the areas of the craft itself, and various areas of the terrain and sky. With the precision of thread-thin lasers, what appeared as single crystals or grains in the emulsion of the targeted areas were projected to a very large size for in-depth study and comparison, searching for overlay and distortion that shouldn't be there if these photographs were taken as described. Four-by-five-inch color transparencies were produced of these key regions, then they were digitized, allowing them to be entered into a Grinnel image processing computer system of 256-by-256 screen resolution. The transparencies of the actual structure of the emulsion represented areas as small as one twenty-five-thousandth of an inch. As the various examination techniques were applied, the visual symptoms which typically indicate overlays, superimpositions, rear projections, and other dark room special effects techniques were not found in either of these internegatives.

It wasn't long before technology had advanced again, almost instantaneously quadrupling its capabilities as a tool in image processing and analysis. Four times the level of detail accomplished by previous systems could now be enjoyed using the new computers, which were now coming of age. The number of potential shades or tones of light and color now recognizable and producible by these systems were grossly multiplied above the level previously seen. This jump forward in technology allowed much finer details of an image to be perceived and studied with greater accuracy. Paralleling this quantum leap was the development of image identification, analysis, and computer software by various high-tech research facilities and manufacturers. These were the written programs that provided the substantial thinking power to the computer hardware which allowed the internegatives to be studied further.

The exhaustive search to uncover just one bogus Meier photograph was now entering its third year without any success—but the search would continue…with the same results.

By the time testing was reinitiated in 1980, technology had once again advanced a major step forward in its precision and capabilities. The computer image processing systems were now capable of 1024-by-1024 detail resolution, creating an unbelievable 1,048,576 possible pixels, or divisions of an image. Thousands of different shades or tones of light were now possible to perceive and reproduce accurately in these twentieth-century systems, allowing for more detail to be seen in the photographic images than was actually necessary. Software, too, had advanced, greatly adding to the analysis capability. The Library Image Processing Software Package, the Cosmic Software Package from NASA,

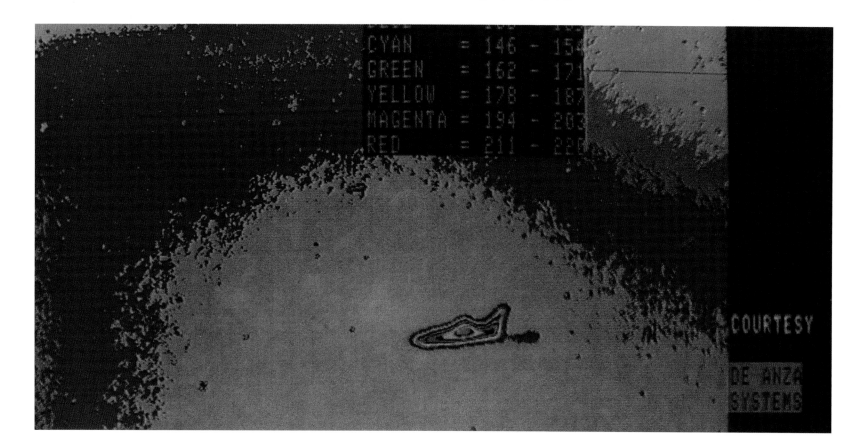

April 14, 1976, 16:11 hours
Location: Schmarbuel
The continuation of the computer's point of view of the "jet-fighter scene" page 38–39. Here the image of the Swiss Mirage fighter has been enlarged to once again focus attention to the red field of particles that are seen enveloping the craft. The jet exhaust is visible, amplified by infrared.

SOBOL Edge Enhancement, and a number of mathematic exponential formulas defining program routines from various specialists immensely expanded the learning power of the Meier photographs. The images were literally being taken apart piece by piece and layer by layer.

The computer image processing system selected at this time to continue the research was the equivalent to those used for reproducing and analyzing the photographic images beamed back to Earth from the Voyager mission to Jupiter and Saturn. High science was no longer interested in finding the nonexistent string holding up the model; instead the concentrated effort was centered on light intensity values with the help of false color mapping and high and low band pass filtering. Contour identification routines were being utilized to determine the three-dimensional, two-dimensional, or single-dimensional nature of the photographs and their objects based upon the histogram. This became exciting research, for soon new light properties previously unseen began to surface in rapid fashion. In one photograph coded the "snow scene," a series of "hot spots" were detected with what appeared to be a corona or "aura" surrounding the beamship. In the "jet-fighter scene," an energy field was discovered emitting from the craft that enveloped the Swiss Mirage as it made its pass on the variation type-3 beamship (see pages 58–59). Controversy would rage over the energy field find, with the detractors arguing that it was only "computer noise." But the argument was flimsy due to the proportioned path of the field, which is seen leaving the beamship in an organized manner to envelope the Mirage, then returning to its point of origination, the craft. There were also statements from a mechanic stationed at a Swiss military base who indirectly supported the photogrammetric find. It was reported that one of the fighters had returned to base with its electrical and fire control system completely melted out. It had required the changing of several "black boxes" to get the fighter operational again. The incident occurred at Schmarbuel in April of 1976.

For the past six years, the Meier photographs have undergone the most detailed and extensive analysis that science has had to offer. The radar-mapping techniques used for the red planet, Mars, were applied to the photographs to determine overlay and paste-up and no deception was found. The edge of the beamship was scrutinized by the same edge enhancement package employed in the examination of the rings around Saturn. The negatives were digitized with the same microdensitometer used on the Pioneer space mission, and still no deception was found!

And so it went. Even as this book goes to print, analysis of the photographs continue as science investigators probe for knowledge into the most spectacular, yet controversial photos of our time. As one prominent scientist put it, "Whether the case is real or not no longer matters, because the investigation has led us into the discovery of new techniques in the field of optical science that works. And it is this knowledge gained that is priceless in nature."

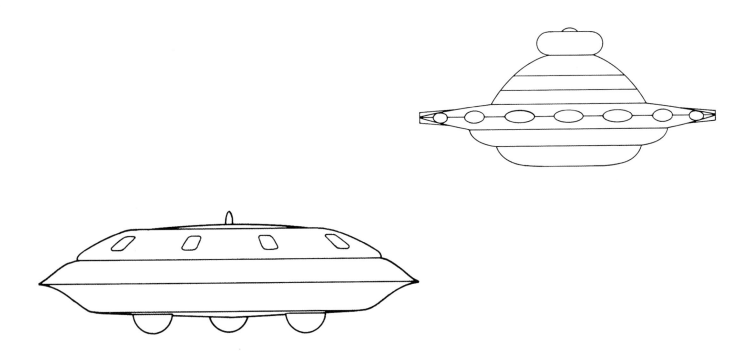

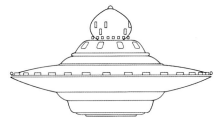
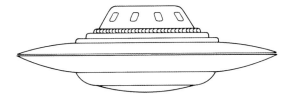

The Unexplained

"A wonder is merely the spiritual force exercising perfection, but, all too often, the human conceals a wonder behind a mysterious veil because he lacks any possible logical explanation."

—**Semjase**, Pleiadian cosmonaut, 1977

July 9, 1975
Location: Fuchsbuel-Hofhalden, near Wetzikon
It was here that Semjase flew one of the second variation beamships slowly around a large *Wettertanne* ("weather pine") so that Meier could get better pictures. One of a series of many pictures showing the spacecraft beside, behind, and in front of the tree. Shortly after the filming, the tree disappeared. The Pleiadians said they had only changed its "time."

"There was the door to which I found no key, there was the veil through which I might not see."

—**Omar Khayyan**

The Meier experiences have spanned a period of eight years, including two distinct, yet separate, worlds of reality. One world involves our normal everyday chemical-physical sphere of being that adheres to the natural laws of our physics in our three-dimensional world. Supporting these natural laws and the subsequent encounters of Meier's is a massive amount of hard evidence gathered during the course of the investigation. And it is this evidence that tends to support the validity of the Pleiadian contacts. But the events have also manifested another world of unchartered proportions that defies our physics and is indefinable to our logic. Within this new dimension comes the challenge of age-old traditions in religion, science, and numerous other accepted laws that we had known to be true. We refer to it as the unexplained for it cannot be investigated in the purest sense due to either a lack of understanding or hard evidence. However, the unexplainable is nothing new to the serious scholars of ufology, having surfaced in countless cases worldwide, lending credence to the idea that it seems to "come with the territory" when one confronts what the Japanese refer to as "the most impenetrable mystery of our time."

Unfortunately, the Meier case is not an exception to this curious rule, as there were numerous examples and countless demonstrations of the unexplainable phenomena. But to ignore or eliminate it from the investigation would be as much of an injustice as it would be to prematurely reject Meier's experiences because they contained the extra-physical side to the contacts. To find that personal level of what one knows to be true, believes to be true, and can prove to be true is indeed a difficult path.

"Something that has never been experienced is always considered a great mystery."

—**Semjase**, Pleiadian cosmonaut, 1977

On July 9, 1975, at Fuchsbuel-Hofhalden near Wetzion, the Pleiadians agreed to participate in a unique photo session that allowed Meier the opportunity to take a series of photographs depicting comparative references. The unprecedented demonstration involved a seven-meter variation type-2 beamship, which hovered over, behind, and in front of a large Wettertanne (weather pine). The experiment was designed to give Meier better "photo-proofs" by filming a known object (tree) with an unknown object (beamship) in the same photograph. It was so successful in presenting comparative references that the flange of the rim of the spacecraft spread the branches when the ship came in close to the tree. (The panoramic view of the scene including the Pfaffikersee [lake] in the background is seen on pages 160–161.)

June 26, 1975
Location: Aboard a Dal Universe spacecraft
This photograph has erroneously been reported by others as a picture of Semjase. This confusion began in 1975 when the first articles on the case were written by lesser-informed individuals and has continued to this day. There are in fact no photographs of the Pleiadian cosmonaut Semjase. Meier said this was a photograph of Asket, a cosmonaut from the Dal Universe who first had contact with Meier in India in 1964 and helped him prepare for the Pleiadian contacts that would occur eleven years later.

Very little is known about the relationship between Meier and Asket in India in 1964 and the "training period" that preceded the Pleiadian contacts, leaving a deeper mystery of the Dal-Pleiadian alliance and their association with each other. However, one thing is known: the Meier family photo album contains numerous old but clear photographs of luminous balls of light and disc-shaped objects flying singularly and in formation above Kutab Minar, Mehrauli, New Delhi, Dog Hill, and the Ashoka Ashram on Gurgoan Road. One spectacular photograph shows a disc-shaped object hovering over the Ashoka Ashram that Meier identifies as Asket's craft. Another photo shows eight unidentified double-sphere objects in formation over the New Delhi railway station.

June 25, 1975
Location: Berg-Rumlikon
This photograph was taken by Meier from within Semjase's beamship. Looking through a window, he photographed two other beamships in formation as the three ships prepared to leave on their journey. It was on this flight that Meier renewed his friendship with Asket after an eleven-year absence.

The photographic experiment was not without abnormal consequences, for one of the strange effects observed was that the top of the tree glowed in the dark for some time afterward. Then shortly after the demonstration, the giant Wettertanne ceased to exist, disappearing without a trace! No radiation measurements were made at the time due to lack of equipment. No follow-up gamma radiation detection was made due to muddy, impassible roads in to the area at the time the equipment was available (1982).

When Meier queried the cosmonauts about the matter, they explained that the tree had been removed because it had been contaminated by a harmful radiation leak from their beamship. However, it was explained that the radiation leak was only dangerous to certain plant life and there was no need for Meier to worry. When pressed for more details the cosmonauts simply stated that they had only changed the Wettertanne's "time." Shortly thereafter, the Pleiadians replaced the beamship with variation type-3, thus eliminating future problems with radiation leaks.

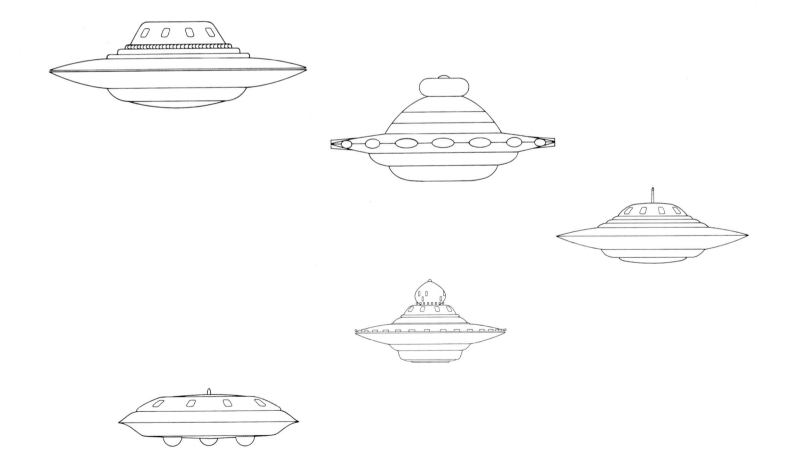

Awakened from a sound sleep by an uneasy feeling, Meier felt drawn outside. It was 02:00 hours and as he walked into the cool night air, he was startled to see an enormous blinding ball of light that was turning night into day. He ran back inside the farmhouse to grab his camera and flashlight, and when he returned, the ball of light had been joined by an unknown object equally intense and bright that moved slowly over the parking area adjacent to the house, shrinking and expanding in shape and size. Meier took several photographs, and this seemed to attract the object, which moved closer to him. Frightened, he dropped his camera and went for his flashlight, pointing it toward the object, but then, without warning, the unknown object shrank in size and shot a beam of light back at him. Meier was shaken!

Meier felt that there was a form of higher intelligence guiding the strange object as he repeatedly tried to make telepathic contact—there was no response. He tried verbal contact, and once again there was no recognition to his strained efforts. It was almost dawn when the pulsating object moved west over the valley below the farm, bathing the area in a brilliant radiance, and then finally disappearing as the morning sun began to appear.

The whole incident had been a chilling experience for the Swiss farmer, because in this instance he was no longer a contactee in his comfort zone but instead a man who had come face-to-face with an unknown phenomenon in the middle of the night.

There were numerous examples of the extraterrestrial power and intelligence when dealing with Meier. Their abilities to transcend space and time, remove and reshape matter at will, were extraordinary manifestations that they continually explained in oversimplified terms. Eventually, those close to the contactee began to notice gradual but significant changes developing in his personality, as he seemed to absorb and comprehend greater amounts of information on almost every subject. One of the most important observations, other than his increased awareness and sensitivity, was in the area of prophecy: advanced knowledge pertaining to futuristic events. These revelations and predictions knew no boundaries, encompassing everything from major political and religious upheavals to macabre deaths of powerful world leaders. However, Meier was adamant in explaining that he had no psychic powers and that he was only receiving the advanced information from the Pleiadians.

Many of the predictions came in the area of natural disasters such as major earthquakes and climate-changing volcanic eruptions. But one of the most profound prophecies involved the United States and its Voyager space probes to the greatest of our Sun's children, Jupiter. What was truly amazing was the fact that the uneducated farmer's notes reflected a detailed conversation held with Semjase years prior to the Voyager missions. It was stated that two new worlds, one of ice (Ganymede) and one of fire (Io) would be found on the surface of these moons in orbit around Jupiter by the Voyager cameras and the findings would be documented sometime in 1979. It was also predicted that the Voyager program would discover three and possibly four new moons in orbit around the giant planet (see *Astronomy* magazine, May 1979). The Pleiadian information to Meier was technically correct, for in October

of 1979, approximately three years after his predictions" the fourteenth moon was found from the Voyager II photographs taken in July of the same year. Then six months later, an unexpected announcement from JPL in California revealed that the fifteenth and sixteenth Jovian moons had been found on photographs taken by Voyager I on March 5, 1979. It was noted that the sixteenth moon was very difficult to detect because it was only twenty-five miles in diameter and appeared as a small black dot against the massive Jupiter surface.

In volume I, the Vega connection was never contemplated as a prediction, only statements of fact taken from the Pleiadian dissertations concerning their ancestor's exodus form the troubled motherland of Lyra, to colonize brave new worlds in the Pleiades, Hyades, and Vega. But prophetic it became! See the August 22, 1983, edition of *Newsweek*.

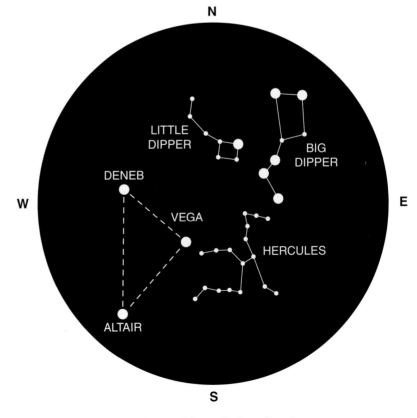

Finding a New Solar System

March 26, 1981
Location: Sekar Durchstolen
This photograph and the one on page 168 marked the first photo sessions allowed by the Pleiadians since 1976. The five-year moratorium on "photo-proofs" was enacted due to their concern of Meier's welfare and the repeated misuse and abuse of the original photographs. Over eight hundred photographs were taken between 1975 and 1976, but only a few remain today. This new beamship, designated variation type-6, was the most advanced of the Pleiadian technology. It has many new features including propulsion that allows it to make the hyper-jump between the Pleiades and Earth in seven minutes, instead of the original travel duration of seven hours.

The Experience Continues...

Afterword: Looking Back

It's been over four decades since we first heard of the Pleiadian contact case. So much has changed in the world since then. UFOs are now called UAPs, which is the acronym for unidentified aerial phenomena. In some parts of the world, such as Mexico, sightings are almost an everyday occurrence. More groups dedicated to research and investigation have organized, and the populace is not so hesitant to share their stories.

Technology has expanded rapidly, and today we can sit down at a laptop and create and manipulate an image that would be close to the photographs we first saw back in 1977. Scientists are more receptive to the possibility of other worlds visiting ours, although there is still a hesitance from some to openly state their opinions for fear of ridicule. Several governments have openly and actively begun releasing old information on the subject and have formed committees to publicly gather new information.

In the United States, we have gone from Captain Eduard J. Ruppelt's findings in a 1956 report that contained significant evidence supporting the existence of intelligence-guided spacecraft operating in American air space to televised congressional hearings on the topic. Although there have been releases of previously suppressed information on the subject, there are those that contend that the majority of sightings and experiences are either bogus or caused by some natural incident and, should these observations be valid, the aerial unknowns should be feared.

When volume I was originally released, we were surprised by its international impact. By invitation, on May 6, 1980, the book and its subject was officially presented in a special five-hour session before the prestigious members of the House of Lords in London, England, thus achieving a credible dimension of acceptance. This outstanding event was soon followed by formal inquiries from other foreign bodies for a qualitative exchange of this and other major UFO information and data. The inquiries alone were staggering in consequence, for when was the last time any book, especially a photo-journal about UFOs, was responsible for bringing together opposing polarities for the sake of a meaningful exchange of knowledge?

During our investigation, we journeyed to Switzerland on eighteen different occasions and spent over three hundred days living at the Meier farmhouse interviewing witnesses from all walks of life, collecting hard evidence, and observing the contactee Billy Meier, his family, and friends. We discovered early their warmth and sincerity and came to appreciate the openness of their unbridled feelings when it came to discussing the experience. To them, everything else was incidental and relatively unimportant, including the ever-present question pertaining to the reality of the many experiences for they had already established their own level of truth. We took full advantage of their offer of free reign into their private world and we had to concede that there was no evidence uncovered that indicated deception.

I'm often asked if I regret the involvement of our time, energy, and money spent on an intangible subject like this. My answer has been and always will be a definitive, "No, I do not regret one bit of it."

There were certainly times when we felt frustration, such as when Marcel Vogel, a research scientist at IBM, claimed that some of the metal samples he had been analyzing "disappeared" from his shirt pocket. Or the time we were filming the analysis of the sounds made by the craft and the lab security team demanded everyone remove anything that would identify the laboratory we were in.

There were, however, many courageous individuals who stepped forward and put their name and their reputation on the line. Jim Dilettoso, Marcel Vogel, Nils Rognerude, Steve Ambrose, Rob Shellman, John McVey, David Froning, and Alan Holt are but a few who openly applied their scientific knowledge and expertise to this investigation.

In the ensuing years after our initial visit to the Swiss farmhouse of Eduard "Billy" Meier, the Pleiadian contact case created rabid controversy. Are Meier's claims real, or are they false? Were the photographs, sounds, and metal samples manufactured? Were the witnesses coerced? Or did the experiences unfold as the contactee said?

I find it interesting that this case, and many others, are attacked and deemed not credible by those who never examined the material or spoke with the individuals they so easily dismissed. Very few of them contacted us to review the material evidence, even though they claimed to be investigators. They wanted us to send the evidence to them, which we declined. We knew that wouldn't make us popular with the groups, but too much of the physical material had already vanished from the Meier farmhouse, and we didn't want to lose more. Then there were those who, for whatever reason, found it necessary to label, deny, and excoriate people they did not know along with documentation they had not examined, much less studied extensively.

It was no wonder that many of the labs and scientists didn't want their name attached to a subject that was considered at that time to be "fringe science" and taboo in most circles. Inevitably someone would characterize the science in a negative way to sully the work and reputation behind it. I've often thought that at times the UFO community was its own worst enemy. Instead of doing their level best to work together to learn from the mountains of evidentiary materials and reported sightings and encounters, they squabbled over it.

We felt the evidence needed to be scrutinized by all sides, but fairly and based on fact, not assumption or straight-up falsehoods. Differences of opinion should be welcomed as a form of expanding one's knowledge and understanding. A hearty discussion that illuminates diverse views only broadens one's perspective. But an investigation cannot be led by opinion. It has to be directed by evidence, no matter what course that may take.

Although in the beginning Lee expected to be able to quickly dismiss the entirety of the case, we ended up with a neutral position. We decided not to prove or disprove it but to just present what we had found. As the initial analysis of the evidence supported the claims, we decided to investigate as thoroughly as possible and to present the results so that people could reach their own conclusions. We felt that the determinations they reached shouldn't be muddled with misleading accusations but should be fact-based. It was for that reason that we reached out to scientists and specialists from various disciplines. We were fortunate to have contacts that had associates that ranged from audio engineers, metallurgists, and photogrammetric analysts to authorities in special effects.

We brought in Wally Gentleman, a British-born Canadian cinematographer and founder of the Montreal-based SPEAC, or Special Photographic Effects and Allied Crafts. An Academy Award winner, he built the model spaceships for Stanley Kubrick's *2001: A Space Odyssey* in 1968. Gentleman studied the pictures and movie footage and determined that a one-armed man, with limited finances, no assistants, and no background in the expertise that was required could not have produced the images.

In a recent conversation, photogrammetric analyst Jim Dilettoso described his efforts this way: "We scouted the best research equipment of that era and then recruited the best experts of that era to examine the evidence and report their findings."[1] Jim's initial work, found in this book, also brought in many other experts in the field such as Robert Post of JPL's photo laboratory. Post stated, "From a photography standpoint, you couldn't see anything that was fake about the Meier photos. That's what struck me. They looked like legitimate photographs. I thought, 'God, if this is real, this is going to be really something.'"[2]

Dr. Michael Malin, principal investigator for the Mars Orbiter Camera on NASA's Mars Global Surveyor spacecraft at Malin Space Science Systems (MSSS) in San Diego, California, also analyzed Meier's photographs. He stated, "I find the photographs themselves credible, they're good photographs. They appear to represent a real phenomenon. The story that some farmer in Switzerland is on a first name basis with dozens of aliens who come to visit him—I find that incredible. But I find the photographs more credible. They're reasonable evidence of something. What that something is I don't know." Malin also said, "If the photographs are hoaxes then I am intrigued by the quality of the hoax. How did he do it? I'm always interested in seeing a master at work."[3]

Rob Shellman, a sound engineer with a secure facility in Groton, Connecticut, was intrigued by the complexity of the audio recordings made of the beamships. He determined that an electrical AC source was not used to create the sounds—50 or 60 Hz frequencies are common electrical outlets and Shellman determined, "If the device that generates the sound was an electric motor or machine the line frequencies would be evident. No such frequencies were detected."[4]

Shellman was one of a number of audio engineers that analyzed the recordings of the beamship sounds. They all determined that the sounds were unique. Their findings concluded that there were at least thirty or more discrete frequencies in a random and constantly shifting mix that ranged from 4 to 2170 Hz but varied on average between 470 and 1452 Hz. The amplitude of these frequencies and the wave shape was constantly changing in a random, periodic rhythm that caused a characteristic beat.

Steve Ambrose, the sound engineer for Stevie Wonder and the inventor of the Micro Monitor radio set and speaker that fit inside Wonder's ear, analyzed one of the recordings. Not only was he unable to duplicate the sounds with synthesizers, he found the sounds created totally unique patterns on a spectrum analyzer and on the oscilloscope.

The wave patterns observed in the oscilloscope showed a constant and random shift in frequency, in which the principal waves of all frequencies came together in perfect synchronization, only to travel at the next moment in different directions and stages, thereby generating different patterns. Then they gradually expanded until, for a brief period of time, they formed a mutually precise and evenly distributed pattern, only then to shift and change patterns— although these changes appeared to be random and were not repeated in a particular order and they seemed to appear in a geometric relationship to one another.

There was a lot of speculation that the audio might be relative to the craft's propulsion. That remains conjecture and quite possibly beyond our scope of knowledge or understanding at this time. But it made us wonder about propulsion.

We consulted several astronautical engineers about propulsion. Dr. David Froning had worked at McDonnell Douglas and spent years in highly classified military defense. Froning was curious about Meier's account of tachyon propulsion, which was at that time in its infancy and a topic that only interested theoretical physicists. Froning told us that he felt there were "breakthroughs in understanding possibilities and ways for traveling faster than light from Billy Meier's accounts."[5]

Marcel Vogel was a research chemist for IBM, held thirty-two patents, and had invented the magnetic disk coating memory system used in IBM disk memories. He was also a specialist in the conversion of energy inside crystals. Utilizing the most current optical microscopic equipment available at that time, he analyzed the metal samples that Meier claimed were from various stages of the creation of the skin of the ship.

Through the lens of a scanning electron microscope, he determined, "Each pure element was bonded to each of the others, yet somehow retained its own identity." At a magnification of five hundred times he discovered thulium was contained in the metal fragment and stated, "Thulium exists only in minute amounts. It is exceedingly expensive, far beyond platinum, and rare to come by. Someone would have to have an extensive metallurgical knowledge even to be aware of a composition of this type."

Vogel's final analysis stated, "With any technology that I know of, we could not achieve this on this planet! And I think it is important that those of us who are in the scientific world sit down and do some serious study on these things instead of putting it off as people's imagination."[6]

That's not to say that the scientists did not have their reservations about the case. After examining and finding no manipulation or fakery, many could not accept that actual face-to-face contacts had taken place. The scientists we spoke to couldn't explain or disprove the evidence, but they couldn't accept the story behind it.

I realize that unless and until a person has an encounter of their own, there is nothing that can convince them of another's experiential validity. Even as an investigator that spent seven years of my life focused on these events, I can't say that I am 100 percent convinced they were authentic as they were described to us. I can say that the analyzed physical evidence combined with state-of-the-art technology of the day tends to support Meier's claims.

One of the most intriguing pieces of evidence was discovered after *Contact from the Pleiades*, volumes I and II, were originally published. During one of our visits to the farm, all of the rabbits suddenly died from an undetermined cause, which seemed odd. We also knew that Meier had been suffering persistent chest colds and other health issues as we had arranged for various natural medicines to be delivered to him. We wondered if the rabbits' deaths and Meier's health problems could be due to something related to his experiences.

Thom Welch contacted a representative of Wild Heerbrugg who agreed to bring in equipment that could measure the gamma radiation in the area and compare it to standard background levels. Meier's moped, belt buckle, pistol, and all of the contact sites, including the earliest, registered well over 100 keV, or one thousand electron volts. They were such high readings that the operator wanted to call in the Swiss Federal Nuclear Safety Inspectorate, which, at the behest of Meier, we talked him out of.

Thulium had been detected in the metal samples from the craft and thulium emits gamma radiation but it is minimal—with a short half-life of about one hundred twenty-eight days—and only when it's bombarded with neutrons. There were no natural sources for such an exchange to occur.

We learned that gamma rays pass completely through the human body and can cause damage to DNA and tissue. Although we couldn't make a direct correlation to the rabbits' demise or Meier's health issues, it was a possible link that the contactee did not want to pursue. Fortunately, we chronicled the information in the documentary film *Contact*.[7]

The witnesses were intriguing to us because they had a mixture of stories that sometimes overlapped. Although no one but Meier was present during the contacts, some had seen the craft, some had heard the beamship, some had seen landing tracks, some had seen unusual lights that moved erratically through the skies, and some had been present when Meier "disappeared" or "reappeared' before them. Lee had an experience like that while he was working on the roof with Meier. They had been talking, and when Lee turned to ask a question, Meier was gone. He hadn't used the ladder, which was positioned directly in front of Lee, and there was no place to hide on the steep rooftop. Hours later Meier returned, casually walking down the road. There was no logical explanation for it, but it happened.

One witness from Germany, Herbert Runkel, described to us one of the many events he witnessed. It had started to rain while Meier was reportedly away at a contact. The group of people waiting for his return stayed in the car, avoiding the downpour that continued for well over an hour. Suddenly Meier emerged from the forest, mostly dry with raindrops just beginning to saturate his clothes. No one present could explain how the contactee avoided getting wet.

On more than one occasion, we, the investigators, became the witnesses to the phenomenon. Throughout the years of our investigation, Lee and I often stayed at the farm in a small camp trailer next to the house. While we were there, we saw things we couldn't explain. Many nights Meier would take off on his moped or the small tractor and be gone for hours before returning to tell us about his most recent contact. On one such night, after Meier had taken the tractor down the road into the forest, we witnessed a light that illuminated literally everything. It was a blue-white light that had no visible source and cast no shadows throughout the forest, not even beneath the branches of the towering conifers.

Once, while we were filming with Jun Ichi Yaoi and his Nippon Television crew, we experienced another anomaly associated with this case. It had been pouring rain for two days, and everything was thoroughly soaked. Meier told us he had walked to a contact site the night before, been taken aboard, and had been dropped off afterwards in a different area.

While filming, we tracked Meier's footsteps in the mud to a clearing down the road that was surrounded by enormous spruce trees. There, the deep impressions of his footprints simply vanished. There were no other tracks of any type in the area and there was no logical explanation for the disappearing footprints.

The various forms of evidence were significant supporting aspects of the case but other elements had to be considered, too, including the contactee and those around him. We had already scoured the farm and surrounding area for models and equipment that could have been used to manufacture the evidence. We found nothing.

As we were just getting into the initial phases of the investigation, we met with Stanton Friedman, nuclear physicist and world-renowned ufologist. He had seen the photographs from the Pleiadian and knew Meier claimed to have contact with the beings when we met with him at Col. Stevens's residence in Tucson. Friedman was candidly blunt in his evaluation of the case. He said that the case might be interesting to look into but his concern was that a cult of enthusiasts would form around Meier. That, in his estimation, would taint the case.

We saw this element early on and watched it grow over the years. People from all around the globe came to visit Meier. Many of them viewed the contactee as a sort of messiah, someone who could solve all problems of the world and save them. They were from various career paths, and they seemed to be attracted to something they deemed unique and greater than themselves. Since Meier was one of the very few contactees of the time, he fit that need.

The thing that Thom, Lee, and I learned was that Meier was human, with human faults and imperfections. Even if he was a contactee, he was no different than any of us. He had his moods, his ups and downs, and, as his recognition and fame grew, we saw him become assertive. His ego, which we all have, was being fed. That was something we could understand. He had spent years trying to share his story with people, and now that they were listening, he felt vindicated. We often discussed and wondered about the possibility that we, through our investigation and subsequent release of books and documentaries, fueled some of those changes, and looking back, we probably did. It was not intentional, but we made the case as much about the uniqueness of the man as we did the evidence.

In the initial phases of the investigation, we saw a simple man, calm and extraordinarily patient with the repetitive questions coming from visitors to the farm. He seemed intent on proving his experiences to each and every one he met, yet he did not freely expound on anything unless he was asked. Human nature, with its natural curiosity and hunger for information, saw people demanding more and more of him. They wanted more of his time for conversation and more access to the evidence.

Visitors who arrived day and night disrupted his family life. It was hard for him to have a moment of peace or time to help the children when they had a problem. At times he felt overwhelmed and told us he wanted "to break the contacts."

Kalliope, his wife at the time we were there for the investigation, was always gracious and giving, even though privacy was nonexistent in that household, and we could see the strain of it all on her face. A dark-haired, independent, fiery Greek, she always had a smile and a warm greeting for us despite our invasive investigation. We spoke with her countless times about her experiences, and she openly told us what she had witnessed and believed, as did their three children, who recounted their experiences with the excitement and wonderment of a child.

The marriage eventually broke apart, and Kalliope later said that her husband had made and filmed models of the craft. That statement was made after she and Billy parted ways and, in my opinion and based on what I had seen firsthand, was out of frustration and irritation at her husband, the group around him, and the overall invasion of her life. I think most people would empathize with her.

After all of the analysis of the images and the uniqueness of the other evidential material, we doubted that it had all been a hoax. However, Kalliope did raise some points that we were also skeptical about. We, like Kalliope, were suspicious of the photograph of Asket, the female cosmonaut whom Meier claimed came from the Dal Universe. The woman in the image looked very much like a woman seen on television years earlier. Our team was also doubtful that images purported to be from an earthquake in San Francisco were anything Meier had seen and photographed himself.

The Pleiadian case was a dichotomy with some items that appeared authentic and a few that cast doubt. Why would the contactee fake certain aspects of the evidence while other forms were testing as valid? Logically the two elements were contradictive and will remain one of the unanswered questions.

To the best of our knowledge, Meier has never admitted hoaxing anything. We wondered if those few questionable issues should invalidate the entire case. We didn't think so, even though we had no explanation for the incongruity. Why and how would a one-armed Swiss farmer with a sixth-grade education create both still photographs and movie footage, produce metal samples and audio recordings? Not to mention the hundreds of witnesses, each of whom provided a form of substantiating documentation to his claim. And why would he then turn around and present questionable items as real? Admittedly, some things were confusing, but we continued on with our research.

Many a night we sat in Meier's kitchen, drinking coffee kirsch, asking questions about the contacts and listening as Meier shared stories about discussions he claimed to have had with the Pleiadian cosmonaut Semjase. (Cosmonaut is the term Meier used to describe astronauts, which is why we used it.)

He talked about spiral universes, reincarnation, the Pleiadians and their way of life, along with their history with Earth. He said that after a contact he would return and write out the dialogue that had been exchanged between them. The contact notes are what swayed Col. Stevens and others into believing everything about the case was real and valid. Col. Stevens, who had always been a hopeful but open-minded investigative collector, lost all objectivity.

As an investigator, the best one can do with this intangible type of information is to compare it to other data that the contactee would probably not have access to. There were several things that we could verify from that perspective and many we could not. He had written about a developing hole in the ozone layer when that hole had not yet been discovered. The contactee told us about a trip into space where he saw multiple moons around the planet Jupiter, more than were recognized at that time, and specifically a moon of fire and one of ice, Io and Europa respectively. They also spoke to him about the rings around Jupiter that consisted of dust and sulfur ions. That information was not known until after the twin Voyager spacecraft reached the enormous planet in 1979, well after Meier had recorded notes about his dialogue in 1978. In one conversation around the table in 1979, he told us Josep Tito would die the following year. The president of the Socialist Federal Republic of Yugoslavia did, in fact, die in 1980, a year after that discussion. The contact note pertaining to the death of Tito was dated October 19, 1978.

One of the most compelling instances that support the Pleiadian dialogues happened while we were in Switzerland. The news reported that President Anwar Sadat of Egypt had been assassinated. Meier quickly left the small living room where we had been sitting. He returned minutes later with a large, blue three-ring binder. Turning the pages, he eventually stopped and laid the book before us. He showed us the contact notes detailing that Sadat would be killed during a military parade.

These are just some of the personal experiences we had and correlative information we gathered, but as part of the investigation, the contact notes remain subjective. There were things we were unable to correlate or verify and we noticed that the contact notes sometimes changed with different translators.

One thing that didn't change in the early contact notes was the beauty of the message. Billy often said that when he was with the Pleiadians, he didn't want to return. The peace and love he felt was all consuming, and he always tried to hold onto that energy when he came back from a contact.

According to Meier and the contact notes, the underlying reason for the contacts was to supply documentation that we, "Earth-humans," as we were referred to in the notes, needed "to realize we were not the only thinking beings in the universe." That is one of the primary reasons these volumes are being republished now.

We ended our investigation in 1985, seven years after it began. Evidence had been analyzed in the US, Japan, Canada, and various European countries. No definitive signs of deception were uncovered. Witnesses came and went. Some couldn't explain what they had experienced, and some people eventually decided it wasn't real because there were those weird anomalies that presented a contradiction. There were several that had a falling out with Meier or the group around him and went their different ways, yet those we spoke to still believed the contacts were real.

We wrapped up the investigation convinced something unique had taken place in Switzerland. The preponderance of evidence supported the contactee's claims, although each of us was drawn to a specific aspect or part of the evidence. For Col. Stevens, it was the contact notes: for Thom, it was the high levels of residual gamma radiation that was found at the contact sites. For Lee and I it was the metal and the structuring of it. With all that we learned over the years, perhaps the most valued lesson was that proof is an individual's perception.

No matter how long the investigation had continued, the fact is that no one but Meier knows the absolute truth of the matter. And if the point, whether Meier's or the Pleiadians', was to help humanity wake up to the possibility of extraterrestrial life, it succeeded. With the original publications of volumes I and II and the initial video releases of the *Meier Chronicles*, *The Movie Footage*, *The Metal*, and *Contact*, as well as the documentaries done with Jun Ichi Yaoi and Nippon Television, we were inundated with mail from people wanting more. The case tapped the imaginations and opened the hearts of the millions of individuals who came in contact with it. Yes, there were those who didn't see the beauty and possibilities it presented. That's all right. The point for releasing the books and documentaries was to present what we discovered and to let people find their own interest, or lack of, in the material.

UFOs and extraterrestrial life are truly intangible subjects for most of us. The good news is that today the experiencers no longer have to whisper about their encounters for fear of ridicule and more scientists are finally considering the possibilities even though they understandably still need to protect their reputations. Today, television programs and books are full of stories that indicate we've been visited by otherworldly beings and thousands of individuals have courageously come forward with their experiences. Yet, in my estimation, this amazing and controversial contact case has never been surpassed in the visual and verbal beauty it presented. The sheer amount of documentation, despite the questionable things I've mentioned, is unparalleled, and the heart-opening messages of the contact notes continue to inspire.

As Semjase said, "...All men hold the truth within themselves and must only know this to find it."

—**Brit Elders**,
Arizona, 2024

Notes

1. Jim Dilettoso, email to Brit Elders, August 29, 2023.

2. Gary Kinder, *Light Years: An Investigation into the Experiences of Eduard Meier* (New York: *The Atlantic Monthly Press*, A Morgan Entrekin Book, 1987), 200.

3. Kinder, *Light Years*, 239.

4. Kinder, *Light Years*, 205.

5. *Contact*, directed and written by Laurence D. Savadove, featuring Lee Elders, Brit Elders (Burbank, CA: Phoenix Film Group, 1987), DVD.

6. *The Metal*, directed by Lee Elders (Phoenix, AZ: Genesis III, 1985), DVD.

7. *Contact*, Savadove, 1987.

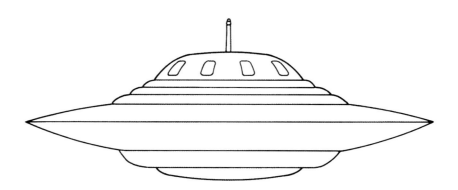